REBUILDING THE TREE

A BLACK GENEALOGY GUIDE TO AI TOOLS

© 2025 T'Malkia Zuri. All rights reserved.

Rebuilding the Tree: A Black Genealogy Guide to AI Tools

First Edition

No part of this publication may be reproduced, stored in a retrieval system, or transmitted in any form or by any means—electronic, mechanical, photocopying, recording, or otherwise—without the prior written permission of the author, except for brief quotations used in critical reviews or scholarly work.

This book is published in both print and electronic formats. The eBook version is licensed for individual use only and may not be shared, distributed, or uploaded to public platforms without express permission from the author or publisher.

This is a work of non-fiction rooted in personal experience, original research, and commentary. While every effort has been made to ensure accuracy, the author assumes no responsibility for errors or omissions. The content is intended for informational and educational purposes only and should not be interpreted as legal, medical, or genealogical advice.

All names, stories, and historical references reflect real people, places, and perspectives from the author's lived experience, cultural background, and research within the Black American genealogy field.

ISBN: 978-0-9961321-0-7

Library of Congress Control Number: On File

Publisher: Griot Publishing House

Cover Design and Interior Layout: T'Malkia Zuri, with the assistance of AI

Author Website: https://griotpublishinghouse.com

Printed in the United States of North America

AI-GENERATED VISUAL CONTENT DISCLOSURE

This book includes AI-generated visual content, such as hand-drawn-style illustrations and infographics, created using AI tools based on custom prompts and artistic direction provided by the author. All visual elements were edited and finalized under the author's creative guidance to ensure cultural accuracy and alignment with the book's message.

Some sections of the text were AI-assisted — including brainstorming, structural formatting, and light editing. However, all core content, personal reflections, research, and final writing were authored and curated by T'Malkia Zuri.

📜 CULTURAL PRESERVATION STATEMENT

This work was created with deep reverence for the Black American lineage — the descendants of the remembered, the returners, the rebuilders. Any misuse, misrepresentation, or unauthorized republishing of this material without consent is not only a legal violation, but a spiritual one.

Before you search, remember who you are. AI is a tool — you are the key. It will only reveal what you're bold enough to ask, and ready enough to remember.

AI Prompt: "Can you help me uncover what my spirit already knows but the records have tried to erase?"

Table of Contents

PART I: GETTING STARTED — FROM SKEPTICISM TO STRATEGY

For those who came to AI with hesitation, questions, or no trust at all. This section builds the foundation, showing you what AI can do — and what it was never meant to replace.

ACKNOWLEDGE: .... **XV**

AUTHOR'S NOTE: **17**

INTRODUCTION: I Didn't Trust the Machine.......**19**

CH 1: Understanding the Landscape — AI, Ancestry, and the Black Researcher's Journey....................................**27**

- **Worksheet:** Your Starting Point...............................**41**

CH 2: Shift the Mindset — You Are the Researcher, AI Is the Assistant...**43**

- **Worksheet:** Prompt Log and Bias Correction...............**50**

CH 3: Building a Foundation Before You Search............**51**

- **Worksheet:** Start With Basics......................................**55**

- **Worksheet:** Research Pep Checklist............................**61**

CH 4: The AI Toolbox — Platforms, Prompts, etc.…..........**67**

- **Worksheet:** My AI Toolbox Planner Pt1....................**74**

CH 5: Letting AI Read What You Can't...........................**79**

- **Worksheet:** Transcription Tracking..........................**86**

CH 6: Show Me the Source — Using AI to Find, Verify, & Cite Genealogy Records with Confidence.................................**87**

- **Worksheet:** Source Tracking.....................................**96**

- **Worksheet:** Conflicting Records................................**97**

CH 7: Using AI to Find the Right Records.....................**99**

- **Worksheet:** AI Search Strategy Grid **112**

CH 8: Upload, Analyze, Organize — Using AI to Extract Key Details from Documents...**115**

- **Worksheet:** Fillable Timeline..................................**125**

CH 9: Power and the Pitfalls of AI................................**127**

- **Worksheet:** Document Your Responses..................**142**

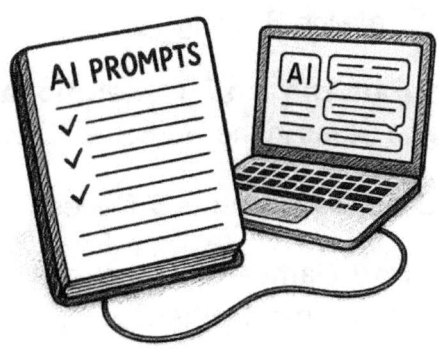

PART II: MASTERING THE PROMPT — ASKING BETTER QUESTIONS TO GET BETTER ANSWERS

This section teaches you how to speak to AI like a seasoned researcher. You'll learn to see through the confusion, prompt with purpose, and decode names, patterns, and lineage clues the records tried to hide.

CH 10: Your First Prompt — Talking to AI Like a Research Assistant...145

- **Worksheet:** Prompt Formula Flowchart................154

CH 11: The Power of the Prompt — Asking Better Questions to Get Better Ancestral Answers...................................**157**

- **Worksheet:** Focused Questions with AI………... 170

CH 12: Guiding the Journey — Using AI to Create Research Plans and Next Steps..**173**

- **Worksheet:** Building AI Research Plan..........................**183**

CH 13: Building a Family Timeline - Blueprint for Clarity.....**185**
- **Worksheet:** Timeline Building....................................**195**

CH 14: Naming Patterns and Generational Codes — Recognizing Lineage Clues in the Names............................**197**
- **Worksheet:** Naming Patterns & Codes......................**211**

CH 15: We Been Had Names — Uncovering Generational Naming Codes and Surname Truths.................................**213**
- **Worksheet:** Name Documenting Chart......................**227**

CH 16: They Speak Like Us But They Ain't Us — Language, Surnames, and the Cosplay of Identity.................**233**
- **Worksheet:** Surname Pattern Analysis......................**244**

CH 17: You Can't Fake This — The Culture Code...............**247**
- **Worksheet:** Culture Code Tracking..........................**257**

PART III: WRITING THE LEGACY — FROM RAW DATA TO ANCESTRAL STORYTELLING

Here, research becomes restoration. Learn how to write the stories your ancestors couldn't, using AI as a co-writer — and your memory as the guide. This is where the healing happens.

CH 18: Beyond the Census — Using AI to Explore Land, Wills, and Probate Records………………………………………**261**

- **Worksheet:** Land and Probate Tracking…………...**273**

CH 19: Using AI to Write Biographies……………………**275**

- **Worksheet:** Build Ancestor Profile…………………..**281**

CH 20: From Snippet to Story — Using AI to Expand Short Clues into Full Ancestral Narratives………………………**283**

- **Worksheet:** From Snippet to Story…..……………**291**

CH 21: Writing Obituaries, and Biographies……………**293**

- **Worksheet:** Ancestor Tribute…………………...**300**

- **Worksheet:** Gather Your Fragments **304**

CH 22: The Living Tree — Using AI to Share, Preserve, and Present Your Research………………………….......…………**307**

- **Worksheet:** Family Tree Planning……………...**316**

CH 23: The Heir's Toolkit — Teaching the Next Generation to Use AI for Black Family Research……………...….....…**319**

- **Worksheet:** Creating an AI Starter Kit **P1**…....…**323**

- **Worksheet:** Creating an AI Starter Kit **Pt 2**...….**325**

CH 24: The Archive We Build Together — Protecting, Sharing, and Teaching What We Found……………....……**331**

CH 25: Why We Rebuild, Remember, and Rise……....**339**

CH 26: The Tree Is Rebuilt — Now What?......................**343**

Rebuilding the Tree Appendices…………………….....**351**

- Appendix A: Source Citations……………….**352**
- Appendix B: Glossary Terms……………….....**356**
- Appendix C: Recommended Books…….…...**359**
- Appendix D/Footnotes……………………….**361**
- List of Source Types……………………………**364**
- About the Author……………………….…...…**367**

WE'VE ALWAYS BEEN THE RECORD KEEPERS

A different spelling doesn't mean a different bloodline.

AI can help match name variants across time, accents, handwriting styles, and clerical errors — bringing fractured names back into one family.

AI Prompt: "Can you find alternate versions of this surname based on regional dialects, phonetic spelling, or past transcription errors?

To the ones they said didn't exist.

The ones reclassified, renamed, and hidden in plain sight.

To the record keepers who remembered anyway.

To the grandmothers who whispered truth in kitchens,

and to the children now waking up to those whispers.

This is for the researchers, the root-workers,

the returners who are rebuilding what was never truly lost.

And to my ancestors —

you left me breadcrumbs in the form of names, places, and dreams.

I found them.

And now I'm leaving a map for the next.

This book is for all of you.

We are the continuation.

We are the legacy.

T'Malkia Zuri

Acknowledgements

This work was not written alone.

It was carried through late nights, whispered meditations, dreams that wouldn't let me rest, and ancestors that wouldn't let me forget. Every page is a reflection of the bloodline I belong to — those who endured, remembered, and passed down enough for me to piece the rest together.

To my oldest son — thank you for opening the door to AI when I was still side-eyeing the machine. Your faith in my voice, your push to evolve, and your patience through my process made this possible.

To every elder who told me stories they thought didn't matter — they did. They became chapters.

To the ones who doubted this path, I thank you too. You helped me sharpen my truth.

To my readers — especially those just beginning your journey: this is more than a guidebook. This is a portal. A declaration. A reclaiming.

To my ancestors — named and unnamed, documented and erased — this is your victory. I am your witness, your record keeper, your returned.

And to the Divine force that guides all truth - the Energy that creates all worlds: I see You. I honor You. I give thanks. — T'Malkia Zuri

BLACK GENEALOGY & AI

This isn't just research. This is *remembrance*. AI can help you search records — but it's your memory, your spirit, and your questions that give those records life.

AI Prompt: "*Can you help me trace my Black ancestral line — through erased names, reclassified identities, and overlooked truths — using every clue the system tried to bury?*"

Author's Note

FOR EVERY BLACK AMERICAN WHO
WAS TOLD THEY HAD NO HSTORY –
THIS IS FOR YOU.

Words carry memory. And in this work, I've chosen each one with intention.

Throughout this guide, you'll see the term *Black American* used often. I want to take a moment to explain why.

I'm fully aware that the term "Black" is evolving. Many of us are waking up to the truth that we were misnamed, reclassified, and disconnected from our Indigenous roots right here on "North" American soil. Today, more of us are identifying as Freedmen, Aboriginal, Copper-Colored, Indian, Amerindian, or FBA (Foundational Black American) to this land — and I honor that shift completely. I've walked that road of awakening myself.

But I also know this: there are millions of our people who still proudly carry the name "Black." Not because they're unaware — but because it's what they've had to cling to in a world that tried to erase them entirely. And there are many more who are just now starting to question, to seek, to remember.

This book is written for all of them.

I use the term Black in this guide not to limit us, but to reach us — wherever we are in the journey. Because if I had picked up a book years ago that said "Amerindian AI Ancestry Toolkit," I would've walked right past it. I would've missed the message. And so would many others.

So let this be a bridge, not a box. Let these words guide you deeper into truth, not lock you into someone else's definition.

We've been renamed enough. But now we get to define, remember, and reclaim who we are — on our own terms.

INTRODUCTION

I Didn't Trust the Machine — Until I Made It Work for Me

I was first introduced to AI in 2020 by my oldest son. I had heard whispers about it — the usual headlines, the fear, the warnings. I wasn't trying to interact with something that claimed to "think." It didn't sit right with me. Mainstream media did its job — painting AI as some rising, soulless system that would one day replace humanity.

But my son shook his head and said, *"Too late. You're already using it — every day. You just didn't know it."*

Still, I wasn't fully convinced. It wasn't until 2021 that I agreed to give ChatGPT a try. I was impressed — quick responses, helpful suggestions, no need to scroll through a thousand irrelevant search results. Before long, I was using it in my web hosting and design business, especially to create social media content with ease. It felt like I had unlocked a digital assistant. I asked, it answered. Simple.

But then came the test that mattered: *"Can this thing help me find my people?"*

I figured, if AI was so advanced, maybe it could help me locate those missing records in my family tree — the ones buried under silence and false labels. But when I asked about Black American genealogy, I hit a wall. The responses were soaked in the same old and tired narrative —

"You came from Africa,"

"there are no records before 1870,"

"check Ancestry.com."

I pushed back. Hard.

I told ChatGPT that we didn't all come from Africa, and definitely not on boats. I explained that many of us were already here. That we were reclassified, renamed, erased, and renamed again. And ChatGPT? It admitted something that stopped me in my tracks:

And that's when it clicked.

> **"I'm only pulling from what's available online — and what the majority agrees upon."**

AI wasn't biased — it was trained on bias.

And if it was going to learn how to talk about us, I was going to have to teach it.

We went back and forth for hours. I challenged everything — from tribal misclassification to the overuse of DNA testing, to the erasure of Black American identities in this land. I'll admit, I got heated. Frustrated. Even angry. It felt like I was arguing with a programmed librarian who had never heard of my grandmother's name. But then something shifted.

I stopped treating it like an authority, and started treating it like a tool.

I began *training the machine* to understand *my truth.*

My history. My tone. My mannerisms. My lineage. And slowly, it began to reflect it back.

The real breakthrough?

One day, I uploaded a death certificate and asked ChatGPT to extract all the relevant info for me. It did it in seconds — clean, organized, and accurate.

That was it. I knew I had to write this book.

This guide, **Rebuilding the Tree: A Black Genealogy Guide to AI Tools**, is not just about tech. It's about *reclaiming memory in the modern age.*

If you're Black American, you already know — your genealogy journey isn't like everyone else's. You're not just dealing with missing records. You're dealing with:

reclassified ancestors,

systemic erasure,

false narratives, and generations of silence.

AI won't do the work for you. But if you know how to train it, question it, and feed it truth — it will become one of the most powerful research tools you've ever had. I created this book to show you how.

Not from theory.

From lived experience. From frustration. From triumph. From tears.

This is your step-by-step map to rebuild what they tried to erase.

And yes, we're using futuristic tools — but don't forget:

We've always been the record keepers.

The ones who know that somewhere in that folded document or misfiled ledger is a story worth finding. **Let's rebuild the tree — not just with names, but with knowing.**

This guide is part of a larger series I've created for those reclaiming their lineage with both truth and discernment. If you haven't already, explore the other books that walk with this one:

Whether you're new to family tree building or deep into census rolls and Freedmen records, this guide will show you how to bring strategy, speed, and spiritual clarity to your work. And if this is your first time engaging with my teachings, I encourage you to go deeper — not just in research, but in remembrance.

- **Black Genealogy Decoded** — A guide to tracing Black American ancestry through census records, including how to interpret racial classifications, migration patterns, and reclassified family lines.

- **Misclassified: The DNA Testing Myth and the Erasure of Black American History** — A breakdown of how commercial DNA testing has distorted our identity — and how to reclaim it without the swab.

- **A Black American Genealogy Guide to Tree Starters** — A powerful two-in-one guide designed for Black Americans determined to reclaim their family history with accuracy and pride. Begin your journey with structured tree building in A Black American Genealogy Guide to Tree Starters, then flip the book to master verification strategies in **Bloodline Verified: How to Vet Your Family Line the Right Way**. Every branch, every record, every ancestor — honored and restored.

- **Revelations of the Remembered: A Message for Black Americans Waking Up in the 21st Century** — This spiritually grounded work speaks directly to those who feel the awakening. It weaves history, divinity, media analysis, and ancestral memory into one powerful call to remembrance.

For those questioning the narratives, feeling the pull of the sun, and seeking their rightful place — this book is both mirror and map.

These works complement each other. Together, they provide a fuller picture — the historical, the practical, and now, the *technological*.

Because we are not just building family trees. We are *rebuilding the record* — and reclaiming every stolen branch.

Now, we're entering a new phase of the work — one that invites technology into the tradition, without letting it replace the spirit.

You're not just entering a new tool — you're stepping into a new way of seeing.

This journey will stretch your thinking, sharpen your skills, and reconnect you with what's always been yours.

Let's begin with intention — and let the ancestors guide the rest.

Part I
Getting Started With Prompts

FEATURED AI TIP

The truth is often scribbled in the margins. AI can help detect handwritten notes, faded labels, or crossed-out names that reveal what the official record tried to hide.

AI Prompt: "Can you analyze the handwritten or altered parts of this record to uncover original names, races, or intentions?"

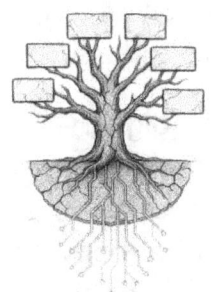

CHAPTER 1

Understanding the Landscape — AI, Ancestry, and the Black Researcher's Journey

What Are You Really Searching For?

Before we begin using tools, platforms, or AI, we need to confront the real question: *What are you actually looking for?* If you say, "I'm looking for my family tree," that's a good start—but it's not the full truth. Most Black Americans aren't just looking for names. We're looking for answers. We're looking for confirmation that our families didn't just appear out of nowhere in the 1870 census. We're looking to understand why records are missing, why names change, and why entire lineages seem to vanish.

This journey is more than digital — it's spiritual. As you begin to understand the role of AI in your research, remember that your roots stretch far beyond the screen. The image below captures the tension and harmony between ancestral memory and modern technology — and the power that emerges when we use both.

This chapter will set the foundation. Because before we start rebuilding the tree, we need to understand why it was broken in the first place.

You're not just researching your family tree — you're preparing to dismantle lies, decode systems, and restore names erased by design.

THE HIDDEN NATURE OF BLACK AMERICAN RECORDS

If you've ever tried to search through census records or death certificates and found yourself coming up empty, it's not your fault. Our records were buried, renamed, misfiled, or never recorded at all. The systems that created these documents were not built to help us find our families. They were created to categorize labor, property, race, and status.

Our people were listed as property, as "mulatto," as "Indian," as "colored," or sometimes not at all. The inconsistencies weren't accidents—they were part of a larger system of reclassification and erasure.

So when you begin this journey, understand that you are not walking a paved road. You're clearing a path through weeds, thorns, and misinformation. You're searching through:

- Records destroyed by fire or flood
- Names that changed with marriage, ownership, or clerical error
- Birthplaces that shift from one document to another
- Ages that vary by decades
- Census takers who couldn't spell or didn't care to

Your job is not just to gather information. Your job is to read between the lines.

THE HISTORICAL MAZE

Let's be clear: The U.S. government didn't create census records to help us find ourselves. These records were built for control — to track, count, and categorize. And for Black Americans, that often meant being listed as laborers, property, or numbers under terms like "Mulatto," "Negro," "Servant," or "Slave."

So, if your great-grandmother disappears in 1880, or your family is nowhere in the Freedmen's Bureau files despite living through emancipation — it's not your fault.

The system wasn't built to preserve your truth. It was designed to preserve theirs. And sometimes, that meant erasing you on paper to justify their policies in public.

These weren't just oversights — they were deliberate acts of omission backed by policy. Generations were reduced to tally marks, or absorbed into categories that told someone else's story. But buried beneath those distortions is still your truth — waiting to be uncovered.

But now, we have something they didn't expect: AI.

Not because it's smarter than us — but because it can sift through data faster than we can. It can spot a reclassified surname across counties and decades. It can clean up messy transcripts, summarize migration trails, and compare patterns in seconds.

If we know how to use it.

WHAT YOU'RE UP AGAINST

Before we dive into AI prompts or platforms, you need to know the terrain:

- **Reclassification:** Your ancestor may be labeled as "Indian" one decade and "Colored" the next. Or they may disappear entirely, only to re-emerge with a new surname.

- **Misspellings:** Names were often written phonetically. "Read" becomes "Reed," "Jonas" becomes "Jones" — and don't get me started on handwriting.

- **Inconsistencies:** Ages might fluctuate by 10+ years. Birthplaces might jump from Missouri to "Unknown."

- **Intentional Gaps:** Entire Black communities were sometimes skipped or under-recorded — on purpose.

When you realize this isn't a perfect record but a *broken map*, you stop blaming yourself.

And you begin to see AI for what it really is: not a miracle, but a **compass** — one that only works if you guide it with *your truth*.

REBUILDING WITH STRATEGY

Don't get it twisted —.**AI won't tell you who your people are.**

It doesn't know Aunt Bessie raised the whole block, or that your grandfather went by three different names depending on the decade and the document. It doesn't know your family moved north to escape Jim Crow or that your cousin was adopted into the tribe.

It doesn't understand why a name might skip a generation, or why some stories were whispered and never written down. It wasn't there when surnames were changed out of fear, or when records were destroyed on purpose. It doesn't carry the weight of silence, or the meaning behind what was left unsaid.

What AI can do is help you piece together fragments.

It can cross-reference, clean up, compare.

It can help you spot the invisible — when you feed it the insight it would never find on its own.

WHAT YOU'LL LEARN IN THIS BOOK

Before you dive into prompts, platforms, or timelines, you need a clear path. This book is your guide — not just for how to use AI, but for how to make it work in a way that reflects your lineage, your language, and your legacy. Whether you're just getting started or have been researching for years, the tools in these pages are meant to help you see what the records tried to hide.

> We aren't just building trees. We are rebuilding a record they tried to bury.

This book will teach you how to:

- Talk to Artificial Intelligence or AI like your research assistant — and get *useful*, culturally aware results
- Create and refine prompts that decode messy records

- Uncover reclassified names, surnames, and patterns
- Build timelines and family stories from raw data
- Use AI as a tool — without letting it overwrite your knowing.

This isn't about letting machines define us. It's about using every tool available to *reclaim* what's ours.

Because we aren't just building trees.

We are rebuilding a record they tried to bury.

And this time, we're bringing memory, spirit, and technology to the table.

SEARCHING VS. REBUILDING

There's a difference between searching for a family tree and rebuilding one. Searching implies that something exists and just needs to be found. But for many of us, the truth is more complex. Our families were broken apart, relocated, renamed, and in some cases, intentionally written out of history.

Rebuilding asks us to start with fragments — a name, a nickname, a place someone once lived. And it requires us to listen just as much for what's missing as for what's there.

It's not just about looking — it's about listening. Listening to patterns, to gaps, to things that don't line up.

And sometimes, the very records we need were never meant for us to find — they were mislabeled, buried, or scattered across counties and courthouses. But we search anyway. We piece together what they tried to erase.

Let this guide reframe your mindset. You are not simply researching. You are reclaiming. You are not just tracing. You are restoring.

WHY THIS BOOK USES AI

Artificial intelligence is a tool. It is not a replacement for your discernment, your instincts, or your lived experience. But it can assist you in incredible ways—*if* you understand how to use it.

Think of AI like a fast, tireless assistant. It can:

- Help you identify patterns in surnames or locations
- Generate timelines from fragments of data
- Translate and simplify historical terminology
- Cross-reference names and dates
- Organize your research
- Suggest alternate surname spellings based on regional dialects and phonetic patterns

But AI is only as good as what you feed it. If you input the wrong name, or if you assume a surname came from a slaveholder without investigating tribal ties, you will get a flawed result.

Use AI to speed up your work—but never let it replace your reasoning.

- ✓ It can highlight clues, but it can't feel the shift in your spirit when a name sounds familiar.
- ✓ It doesn't know when a place name makes your chest tighten or your memory stir.
- ✓ It will never understand the silence in your family tree or why one generation vanished from the page. That's where you come in.

You are the human interpreter.

You bring the cultural memory, the ancestral awareness, the wisdom to know when the records are lying—or just incomplete.

This book uses AI because it respects your time—but it also respects your truth. And when both work together, you gain power, precision, and a process rooted in both strategy and spirit.

And remember — what the tool can't see, your bloodline can feel.

Sometimes a name will leap out, not because it was bolded in the record — but because your spirit recognized it.

Sometimes an unfamiliar surname will call you to dig deeper, not dismiss it.

Trust those moments as much as the data. They are the bridge between machine logic and ancestral memory.

SEVEN QUESTIONS TO GROUND YOUR RESEARCH

Before you enter a search term, before you write your first prompt, ask yourself these seven questions:

1. How did my family identify racially or ethnically over the generations?
2. Are there any family surnames that changed spelling or pronunciation?
3. Are there migration patterns I can trace—county to county, state to state?
4. Are there oral histories of Indigenous identity that don't show up in the records?
5. Do I understand the difference between how my family named themselves and how officials recorded them?
6. Are there names or places that repeatedly show up in family stories, even if they aren't on paper?
7. Did any ancestors live as boarders, servants, or laborers in households under a different surname?

These questions are not just personal reflections—they are critical research strategies.

They will shape your prompts, your keywords, and your expectations.

A Practical Example

```
                                                    State file number:
1. 30 BF BF DECESOFT
                        DEATH CERTIFICATE
1. FULL NAME
              MARY JANE JOHNSON
2. DATE OF DEATH                         3. AGE
         F                                  74
4. ACE                                   8. RACE
                                            COLORED
4. PLACE OF DEATH    A)                  8. COUNTY
    Hospital  Inpatient  ...
7. MARITAL STATUS ...                    12. Ever served in U.S. Armed Forces
   No                                       Yes    No
   New                                   13. OUTSIDE OF TOWN LIMITS?
   Not married                              Yes    No
3. FATHER'S NAME                         14. LOCATION CITY OF TOWN ANESIAFL
          UNNNOWN
15. MOTHERS NAME Prior to first marriage)
          ELIZA MAYFIELD                 23. METHOD OF DISPOSITION
15. INFORMANT
          F. WATKINS
```

Let's say you come across a death certificate. It lists:

- Name: Mary Jane Johnson
- Age: 74
- Race: Colored
- Father: Unknown
- Mother: Eliza Mayfield
- Informant: E. Watkins

You might assume this is a dead end. But it's not. Here's what you do:

1. Calculate Mary Jane's approximate birth year based on her age.

2. Search for Eliza Mayfield in that region, across a range of spelling variations.

3. Investigate the informant—E. Watkins could be a relative, and that relationship might lead to more records.

4. Consider whether "Mary Jane Johnson" was her married name.

5. And lastly, ask AI to help you generate possible census records using these clues. You're not just reading a document. You're decoding it.

Before we go any further, let's ground ourselves. Every researcher's journey begins somewhere — not with perfection, but with presence. You may only have a name, a memory, or a feeling in your spirit that someone is waiting to be remembered. That's enough.

Even if the records are missing, the wisdom is still with you. It's in the foods your family cooked, the sayings they passed down, the way a certain name makes your heart pause. Those are not just sentimental moments — they're signposts.

Don't overlook what's been living in your memory all along. Your awareness, your intuition, and your willingness to slow down are research tools, too.

Before we rely on AI to pull from archives, let's make sure we've pulled from within. The search doesn't start with a record — it starts with you.

[Figure 1] is here to help you take inventory of what you already know and what you've inherited — not just through documents, but through stories, family habits, and the questions that won't let you go. This is your launchpad. Your ancestors already left you clues. Now let's gather them.

Jot down important notes from this chapter:

_____

_____

_____

_____

_____

_____

✳ Figure 1: YOUR STARTING POINT

What do I hope to find in my family research?
_____
_____

What obstacles have I encountered so far?
_____
_____

What surnames or stories have been passed down in my family?
_____
_____

What assumptions am I ready to challenge?
_____
_____

What does rebuilding the tree mean to me?
_____
_____

Figure 1: Your Starting Point — A reflection worksheet to clarify your goals, obstacles, family narratives, and readiness to rebuild.

FEATURED AI TIP

AI is not the expert — *you* are. Let it support your vision, not replace it. Guide it with purpose, correct it when it wanders, and remind it who the story belongs to.

CHAPTER 2

Two

Shift the Mindset — You Are the Researcher, AI Is the Assistant

Before you even type your first prompt, there's one truth you need to anchor deep:

AI isn't your teacher. It's your tool.

You are the one holding the memory.

When you're doing Black genealogy — especially from an Indigenous American perspective — you cannot afford to hand over authority to a system that was trained on biased archives, mainstream assumptions, and historical erasure. You're not here to be led blindly. You're here to **direct the search**.

This chapter is about claiming that role — as the lead researcher, the cultural interpreter, the spiritual descendant. AI can't replace that. But it can help you **accelerate your mission** once you know how to talk to it.

FIRST, SHIFT YOUR MINDSET

AI is only as helpful as the instructions you give it.

It doesn't know your family.

It doesn't know your lineage.

It never heard the hush that fell when certain names were spoken.

It doesn't feel the electricity you feel when you find a familiar county name.

It wasn't sitting at the kitchen table when the old stories surfaced.

That's your role. So, let's break this down:

🚫 Don't Just Say:

"Help me find my great-grandfather."

That's too vague. AI doesn't know who you are, what records

you already have, or what region you're referring to.

✅ Do Say:

"Using this 1900 census transcription, summarize the household information for a man named Isaiah Reed, age 45, living in Lowndes County, Mississippi. Include all household members, their relationship to him, race, age, and place of birth."

Boom. That's a clear ask. You've given it:

- A **source** (1900 census)
- A **focus** (Isaiah Reed)
- A **task** (summarize household)
- A **format** (include names, race, age, birthplaces)

You're not just searching. You're **directing**.

COMMUNICATING WITH AI: PRINCIPLES TO REMEMBER

---

1. **Be Specific, Not General**

    🚫 *"Tell me about Black genealogy."*

    ✅ *"List five challenges faced by Black Americans searching census records between 1870 and 1940."*

2. **Break Tasks Into Steps**

a) First: Ask AI to extract names.

b) Then: Ask it to explain anomalies like age changes or race reclassifications

3. **Always Provide Context**

If you give AI a paragraph from a will, add the year, location, and known surname history.

Context changes *everything.*

4. **Watch for Assumptions**

AI often defaults to mainstream ideas like, *"Your ancestors were likely slaves brought from Africa."*

Redirect it:

> *"Do not assume African origin. Search based on Black Indigenous families in Virginia in the 1700s."*

PROMPT STARTERS TO TRY

Before you get overwhelmed trying to craft the "perfect" AI prompt, pause. You don't have to be a tech expert — you just have to know what you're looking for. The goal isn't to impress the AI — it's to instruct it.

These prompt starters will help you ask better questions, so you can get clearer answers that move your research forward with purpose.

> *"Compare the 1880 and 1900 census records for this family and identify any name or age discrepancies."*

"List potential reasons why a person would be listed as an Indian in 1900 and a Negro in 1910 in Mississippi."

"Generate a timeline for the Reed family based on these events: marriage in 1885, land record in 1892, death in 1913."

"Reformat this Freedmen's Bureau contract into a summary that includes all names, labor terms, and locations."

YOU ARE STILL THE AUTHORITY

AI is impressive — it can read handwriting your eyes can't, and it can speed up tasks that used to take you days. But it doesn't carry the memory — you do.

That's your advantage.

That's your gift.

That's the ancestral code no algorithm can replicate.

You're not just learning how to use a tool; you're learning how to command it.

You are the researcher. You are the interpreter. You are the memory-keeper.

You know the difference between data and legacy — and that's something no machine can ever learn.

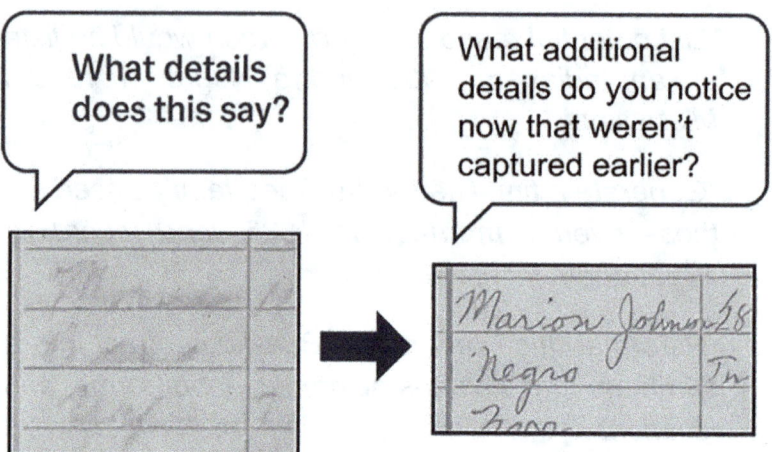

Let the tool serve the legacy. Let the algorithm organize the documents. But let you be the one who brings it all home. Because this isn't just data. It's divine restoration.

AI can trace a pattern — but it can't feel what that pattern meant to the people who lived it.

It never felt the fear behind a name change meant to shield a child, or when a family member was left off the record to protect them.

It doesn't understand what it means to be erased — and still find your way back.

It can't feel the ache of not knowing, or the power in finally remembering. That belongs to you. That's why your role matters even more now — not less. The more powerful the tools become, the more intentional we have to be about how we use them.

✅ AI can help you search faster, but it can't feel what you know

✅ It doesn't carry the weight of that surname — the way it echoes through your family stories, or why that place name makes your chest tighten with memory.

✅ It wasn't shaped by the lullabies, the prayers, or the warnings passed down in your line.

✅ It doesn't carry the weight of what was whispered at the kitchen table or buried in a grandmama's sigh

You're not just learning how to use a tool — you're learning how to command it.

As you begin developing stronger, more effective prompts, it's important to track what works — and where bias shows up. The worksheet sample in **[Figure 2]** gives you a place to log your best AI prompts and document how the system responds, so you can adjust and improve your approach over time.

✳ Figure 2: PROMPT LOG & BIAS CORRECTION WORKSHEET

Save the best search prompts inquiries for future use

Date	Prompt

Bias Correction Guide

Use the example and pointers to correct AI bias

- Specify the bias or issue
- Give context and location details
- Ask AI to avoid assumptions
- Request a rephrased response

Figure 2: Prompt Log & Bias Correction Worksheet This worksheet helps you track your best AI prompts and refine your approach for greater accuracy and cultural alignment. With space for notes, bias alerts, and correction strategies, it ensures your research stays intentional, respectful, and rooted in truth.

CHAPTER 3

Getting Started — Building a Foundation Before You Search

Let's talk about this new tool.

The most important step in Black genealogy is not typing your last name into a search box. It's building a foundation. For us, that foundation goes beyond paperwork — it's built on *clarity, context,* and *consciousness.*

Before you ask AI to trace a lineage or organize your family tree, please make sure you know what you already have, what you've assumed, and what still needs confirmation.

Without this preparation, AI becomes just another search engine. But when you do the groundwork, AI becomes a powerful partner.

START WITH YOURSELF — ALWAYS

The root of every strong tree is a source — and in this case, **you are that source**. Before you search databases or prompt AI for answers, take the time to center your own story. You are not just a researcher; you are a living record. Your life, your memory, your presence carries data no archive ever will.

Write down everything you know about your own life, no matter how obvious it may seem. You'd be surprised what details are forgotten or distorted over time.

Start with the basics:

- Your full name (including nicknames, middle names, and any name changes)
- Your date and place of birth
- Your parents' full names and birthplaces
- Your grandparents' names (including maiden names)
- Known surnames on both maternal and paternal lines
- The locations where your family lived over time — cities, counties, regions
- Family sayings, traditions, or oral histories passed down to you

Then go deeper:

- What do you *remember* about your childhood home?
- What did your elders call each other?
- Were there "forbidden" stories?
- Did anyone speak of land, migration, Indian ancestry, or a place "we used to be from"?

These details may seem personal or unimportant now, but they often hold the **keys to surname variations, regional migrations, and reclassified identities** that AI can work with more precisely.

This may sound simple, but many people skip this step. They jump generations ahead and miss essential clues that could have helped AI generate more accurate results — clues that were in their own memory the whole time.

Start with yourself not just because it's convenient — but because **you are the beginning of the recovery.** You are the record that is still breathing. You're not just using AI. **You are feeding it the truth that only you can provide.**

Before you go looking for ancestors, pause, and turn the lens inward. You are the foundation.

[Figure 3]: Start With Self — The Living Record Behind the Research Worksheet. Before you search databases or prompt AI for answers, start by documenting your own story. The details you provide here will help AI, researchers, and future generations understand your lineage and history with greater precision.

Jot down important notes from this chapter:

_____

_____

_____

_____

_____

_____

_____

✳ Figure 3: START WITH THE BASICS:

Full Name *(include nicknames, middle names, and any name changes)*:

___

Date and Place of Birth:

___

Parents' Full Names and Birthplaces:

___

Grandparents' Names *(include maiden names if known)*:

___

Known Surnames *(Maternal and Paternal Lines)*:

___

Family Locations Over Time *(Cities, Counties, Regions)*:

___

Known Cultural, Tribal, or Religious Identities:

___

Family Sayings, Traditions, or Oral Histories:

___

Were there "forbidden" stories or subjects?

___

INTERVIEW THE LIVING BEFORE YOU SEARCH THE DEAD

Before you start digging through dusty records, talk to the people who are still here.

Your elders are walking archives. Each one holds stories, timelines, and context that can't be found online.

Who to talk to:

- Parents
- Grandparents
- Great-aunts and uncles
- Cousins
- Older siblings
- Long-time neighbors
- Family friends

What to ask:

- What do you remember about our family origins?
- Were there any migrations, moves, or significant events?
- What surnames or nicknames did our people go by?

- Were there stories about being Indian, mixed, or connected to certain lands?
- Do we have old Bibles, photographs, deeds, letters, or obituaries?

Record the interviews (with permission). Keep notes. These details may hold the very surnames or locations you'll need later.

GATHER CORE SURNAMES AND LOCATIONS

Surnames and places are your two anchors in any tree-building process.

Create a two-column tracker:

CopyEdit this chart:

Surname | Location | Time Period

--------------|--------------|-----------------

Reed | Alabama | 1890–1940

Mayfield| Missouri | 1870–1910

Do this for both maternal and paternal lines.

But remember — **surnames can change**. Many Black American families experienced:

- Reclassification from Indigenous to Black
- Surname shifts due to enslavement, adoption, or marriage
- Clerical misspellings and phonetic spellings (e.g., "Jonas" for "Jones")

AI can help find variations — but *you* have to provide the initial patterns.

KNOW THE GAPS AND WHY THEY EXIST

Black genealogy isn't hard because we didn't exist — it's hard because we were erased.

Here are some realities:

- The **1890 U.S. Census** was mostly destroyed by fire.
- **Freedmen's Bureau** records don't cover every state or region.
- "Black" Indigenous families were often **reclassified, renamed, or skipped**.
- **Enslaved people were not named** in most records before 1870.
- Many family members were shipped **out** of America — not into it.

- Midwives and Black doctors often kept private records that were never turned over to state registries.
- Many Black veterans were misclassified or omitted from official military pension and service records, particularly before World War I.

If you know why there are gaps, you stop wasting time looking for perfect records.

CREATE A WORKSPACE OR BINDER

Whether you prefer digital tools or a good old-fashioned binder, set up a research system.

Organize:

- Family group sheets
- Timeline charts
- Notes from interviews
- Historical records
- AI-generated summaries or maps
- Surname variation tables

This will keep you from chasing the same leads repeatedly — and allow you to spot patterns AI might miss.

Before you bring AI into the picture, you need to set the stage. The checklist in **[Figure 4]** outlines the essential groundwork every Black genealogy researcher should complete first — from gathering personal records to organizing surnames and noting down ancestral clues. This is how you prepare the soil before planting the digital seeds.

🟢 Figure 4: RESEARCH PREP CHECKLIST — PRE-AI ORGANIZATION ESSENTIALS

This worksheet helps you gather and organize everything you already have before using AI. Preparation makes your searches more focused — and your results more accurate. Don't rush the process. Lay the groundwork.

✔ **Full name(s) of the person you're researching:**

✔ **Estimated birth year and location:**

✔ **Known parents, siblings, or spouse(s):**

✔ **Any alternate spellings or surname variations you've seen in records:**

✔ **Locations they lived (cities, counties, regions):**

✔ **Key events with rough dates (marriage, death, migration, etc.):**

✔ Any known oral stories or family claims about this person:

✔ What you've already searched or found so far (census, death cert, etc.):

✔ Specific questions you want AI to help answer:

✔ Optional: Notes on gaps, inconsistencies, or conflicting info:

HOW AI HELPS AT THIS STAGE

Once you've laid the groundwork, here's how AI can assist you:

- Create personalized family tree templates
- Summarize interviews or old handwritten notes
- Generate timelines based on birthplaces and migrations
- Identify generational gaps or data inconsistencies
- Help draft prompts for deeper searches

But remember — **AI needs your direction.** If you don't give it cultural context, names with variations, or a timeline to work from, it can't guide you accurately.

Getting started isn't about jumping into records — it's about knowing what to ask, who to ask, and what to collect.

You're not just gathering data. You're gathering *meaning* — the essence of lives lived, paths crossed, and roots that reach deeper than any digital tool can understand alone. From there, your tree will begin to rise.

- ✓ Start with yourself.
- ✓ Listen to the living.
- ✓ Trace the names.
- ✓ Understand the land.

✳ Figure 5: MY RESEARCH FOUNDATION PRE-AI REFLECTION WORKSHEET

Before using AI, it's important to ground your research in what you already know, believe, or suspect. This worksheet helps you clarify your personal knowledge, identify known gaps, and center your research around meaningful questions — not just random searches.

Use this worksheet to capture your own life details, family connections, and questions before introducing AI. It allows you to reflect, organize, and document what matters most — so your search starts from a place of memory, not guesswork.

What do I already know about my family history?

_____

_____

What oral stories or family traditions have been passed down to me?

_____

_____

What questions am I hoping to answer through this research?

_____

What records, documents, or clues do I already have?

_____
_____
_____

What am I unsure about — or what doesn't seem to add up?

_____
_____
_____

Are there any cultural, tribal, or regional identities I should be aware of?

_____
_____
_____

What emotional, spiritual, or ancestral intentions am I bringing to this work?

_____
_____
_____

Figure 5: Before using AI, it helps to clarify what you already know. This worksheet grounds your research in lived memory, family knowledge, and foundational clues.

Don't just store results — store what worked.

AI gets better when you track which prompts gave you the best outcomes. Save your winning phrases, test how AI responds to tricky records, and make notes of any patterns or errors you see.

CHAPTER 4

The AI Toolbox — Platforms, Prompts, and Possibilities

Once you know how to write a strong prompt, the next step is choosing the right tool to deliver it. Not all AI tools are created equally, and not every one of them is built for genealogy. In this chapter, we'll break down the best AI platforms for Black genealogy research, the strengths and limits of each, and how to choose the one that fits your workflow.

This is your toolbox — and it's time to get familiar with the tools inside.

TYPES OF AI TOOLS FOR GENEALOGY

There are three main types of AI tools that can help in genealogy:

1. **Text-Based AI (Chatbots)**

Tools like ChatGPT, Claude, or Gemini are designed to process language. These tools are great for:

- Drafting family narratives
- Analyzing documents
- Generating prompts or research ideas
- Comparing and organizing records

2. **Image Recognition & Optical Character Recognition (OCR)**

Today's Platforms like Transkribus or Google Lens can scan handwritten or printed documents and turn them into searchable text. This is powerful when dealing with:

- Census forms
- Death certificates
- Bible pages
- Land deeds

3. Record Search & Automation Tools

Some Artificial Intelligence (AI) tools automate search patterns across multiple databases (e.g., RecordSeek, MyHeritage AI Record Matching). While they don't always focus on Black history, you can still use them with guided input and customized filters.

Task	Best AI Type	Suggested Tool
Writing a biography of an ancestor	Text-based AI	ChatGPT, Claude
Transcribing a death certificate	Image-to-text OCR	Transkribus, Google Lens
Finding census matches	Automation + filters	MyHeritage, Ancestry AI
Summarizing a family story	Text-based AI	ChatGPT, Gemini
Searching historical newspapers	OCR + search AI	Newspaper.com OCR, GenealogyBank

No single tool does it all. Just like a good researcher relies on multiple sources, you may find yourself using two or three AI tools in a single session.

KEEP IT PRIVATE AND BACK IT UP

Many AI platforms learn from what you input. **Before uploading sensitive data** (like family death certificates, tribal enrollment cards, or private correspondence), **check the privacy settings**.

Use offline tools if needed — or strip identifying info.

And always keep a backup copy of:

- Prompts used
- Data pulled
- Versions of family timelines

AI can help organize, but you are the keeper of your tree.

If you're using ChatGPT, here's how to review your privacy settings:

1. Click your profile icon (usually at the bottom left on desktop or top right on mobile).

2. Go to

   Settings > Data Controls (or "Personalization & Data").

3. Toggle **"Chat History & Training" OFF** if you don't want your conversations used to train the AI.

4. You can also use **Export Data** to download your session history.

Note: When history is turned off, your chats are still processed but not stored or **used to improve** the model.

Don't assume that just because AI feels personal, it's private — always treat your uploads with the same caution you would in a public archive. Remember: once your data is out, you can't control how it's interpreted, copied, or stored — but you *can* control what you choose to share.

HOW TO USE THESE TOOLS TOGETHER

Let's say you found an old family Bible with handwritten notes:

1. Use **Google Lens** to capture the handwriting and convert it to text.

2. Copy that transcription into **ChatGPT** and ask it to help you identify names, dates, and relationships.

3. Use **MyHeritage AI Matches** to see if any of those names appear in census or death record databases.

Suddenly, you've just turned one hard-to-read photo into three leads.

That's the power of layering your AI tools.

RECOMMENDED AI TOOLS TO START WITH

Not all AI platforms are created equal — and not every tool will serve your research the same way. In this chapter, we explore some of the most accessible and powerful tools currently available, and how to use them strategically for Black genealogy work.

Each platform has strengths and limitations, but when used in harmony, they become a full toolbox — not just a hammer. You don't use a wrench to cut wood. And you don't need a giant language model to answer a yes-or-no question. Learn which platform to call on based on the task at hand.

Here's a beginner's list to keep in your genealogy toolkit:

- **ChatGPT (OpenAI)**

Best for natural conversation, summarizing long records, building timelines, and writing ancestor bios in your tone. Be sure to include specific context — this tool responds best when you give it direction.

- **Claude (Anthropic)**

Handles large files like OpenAI. Great for uploading long transcriptions, Freedmen's Bureau reports and/ or pension documents. Claude often provides gentler, more human-like responses with less abrupt tone.

- **Perplexity.ai**

A powerful research assistant. Use this for cross-referencing census facts with public documents, local history, or migration patterns. Its source-linking makes it ideal for double-checking AI output.

- **Google Gemini**

Still evolving, but helpful for basic fact-finding or quick context. Be cautious with assumptions about Black history — this one tends to default to mainstream narratives.

- **Microsoft Copilot**

Integrated into tools like Word and Excel. Use it to reformat data, auto-organize ancestor logs, and summarize spreadsheets. Also works well for generating citation templates inside your documents.

- **OCR Tools (Google Lens, Adobe Scan, etc.)**

Not traditional AI platforms, but extremely important for converting handwritten records into searchable, editable text.

Each of these tools offers possibilities — but only when paired with your direction. Think of yourself as the conductor.

The AI is just the instrument. If you want harmony, you have to lead.

You've now been introduced to the tools — but knowing is not enough. You need to pause, reflect, and decide which ones serve your purpose. The worksheet sample in **[Figure 6]** allows you to document which AI platforms resonate with your research goals, track how they respond, and build a toolbox that's tailored to your legacy work.

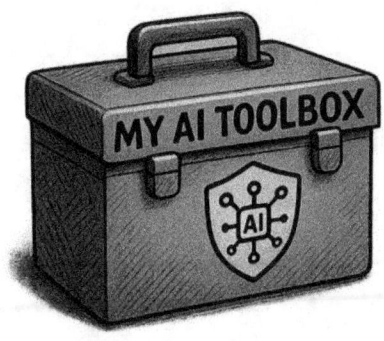

✳ Figure 6: 🧰 MY AI TOOLBOX PLANNER

Use this worksheet to track the AI tools you're using for genealogy — and how each one supports your research. You're not just experimenting — you're building a system.

- **TOOL NAME**: _____

What I Use It For:
_____
_____

Best Prompt or Feature:
_____

Notes or Limitations:
_____
_____
_____

- **TOOL NAME**: _____

What I Use It For:
_____

Best Prompt or Feature:

_____

Notes or Limitations:

_____

_____

_____

- **TOOL NAME:** _____

What I Use It For:

_____

_____

Best Prompt or Feature:

_____

Notes or Limitations:

_____

_____

_____

_____

_____

TECHNOLOGY MEETS ANCESTRAL MEMORY

Technology can't replace tradition, but it **can** serve it.

It doesn't carry the dreams your grandmother whispered while shelling peas. It doesn't feel the heat of homecoming when you read a surname that sounds like a psalm. But with your guidance, it can honor those memories.

When you blend your ancestral knowledge with modern tools, you're not just researching — **you're reactivating memory**. You're turning static names into living legacies. You're pulling forgotten people out of silence and letting their stories breathe again.

Let AI handle the heavy lifting.

Let your intuition do the leading.

Let the platforms support the process — but let **you** be the one who knows what matters most.

Use the tools. But trust your spirit.

Before you choose a platform, it helps to see them side-by-side. Each tool brings something different to the table — and when used wisely, they work together like a well-balanced team. The chart in **[Figure 7]** outlines what each major AI platform does best so you can build your toolbox with purpose.

AI GENEALOGY TOOLBOX
Core Platforms and Capabilities

PLATFORM	STRENGTHS	Chat	Search	Organize	Other
ChatGPT	• Best for dialogue, detailed analysis, writing help	✓	✓	✓	✓
Gemini	• Fast reader. good for long and hanowritten texts	✓	✓		
Bing	• Excellent for real-tiine search results	✓	✓		
Claude	• Large free tier, better at longer uploads	✓	✓		

Figure 7: AI Genealogy Toolbox — Core Platforms and Best Use Cases. This table offers a quick-reference guide to major AI platforms used in genealogy research. It highlights the strengths, cautions, and best use cases for each tool, helping you decide which one to call on for tasks like transcription, summarizing, record comparison, and storytelling.

FEATURED AI TIP

Sometimes a single word in a document can unlock a door. Pay attention to unusual terms, tribal names, land descriptions, or handwritten notes. AI can help you break them down, trace their origins, and connect the dots.

AI Prompt: "Can you analyze this word or phrase and tell me what it might mean in historical or geographic context?"

CHAPTER 5

Transcribing Truth — Letting AI Read What You Can't

One of the most powerful — yet underused — applications of Artificial Intelligence or *AI* in genealogy is transcription.

Handwritten census pages, faded death certificates, and barely legible notes in family Bibles can stop you in your tracks. But with the right AI tool, you can decode those scribbles and extract names, dates, locations, and relationships that change everything.

This chapter is about using AI to make the unreadable readable.

WHY TRANSCRIPTION MATTERS IN BLACK GENEALOGY

A lot of our records were handwritten — by census takers, church clerks, and sometimes family members. Those records:

- Weren't always written clearly
- Used old-fashioned cursive or regional spellings
- Included racial identifiers that shifted across decades

If you can't read them, you can't use them. And unfortunately, many researchers give up too soon.

But don't worry — there's help.

TOOLS THAT CAN READ HANDWRITTEN DOCUMENTS

1. **Google Lens (mobile OCR)**

   Snap a photo of a document, use the tool to highlight the text, and copy it into your notes.

2. **Transkribus (AI Handwriting Reader)**

   Designed specifically for historical records. Upload

an image and let it try to read the handwriting — even in difficult cases.

3. **ChatGPT (with transcription)**

   Once you have the text extracted, paste it into ChatGPT and ask it to:

   - Correct obvious errors
   - Summarize key names or relationships
   - Identify odd terminology or outdated phrases

4. **Photoshop or Canva (enhancing contrast)**

   Sometimes adjusting the brightness or sharpening the image can make a big difference before transcription.

A PERSONAL EXAMPLE

I remember trying to read my great-grandfather's WWI draft registration card. The handwriting looked like scribbles. At first, I gave up. But then I used Google Lens — and while it only got 70% of the words right, that was enough. I pasted the result into ChatGPT and asked for help interpreting it.

What I got back was a full summary — name, occupation, birth date, and even the nearest relative listed. That one card filled in a gap I'd had for years.

That moment taught me not to give up on hard-to-read documents. With the right tools — and the right mindset —

what **looks** lost can still be recovered. And, with the right tools — and the right mindset — even what **feels** lost can still be recovered as well.

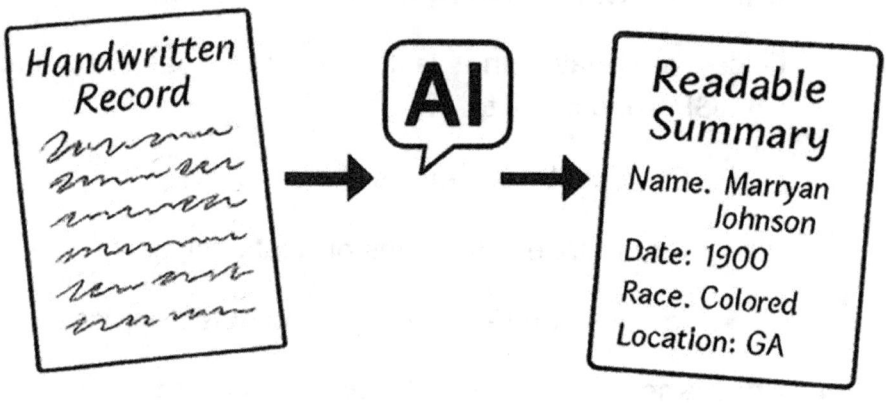

TIPS FOR BETTER TRANSCRIPTION RESULTS

- Crop your image to focus on one section at a time.

- Use grayscale or black-and-white filters to reduce distractions.

- Look for consistent words (like "County," "Negro," or "Widow") and use them to orient yourself.

- Ask AI to correct misspellings and provide modern word equivalents.

- Magnify difficult areas to catch faded letters or old script styles.

- Compare repeated entries (like surnames or town names) to spot patterns and correct errors.

DEALING WITH INCOMPLETE OR DAMAGED DOCUMENTS

Some documents are just too far gone. Torn pages, ink blots, or burn damage can erase valuable names. But don't count them out just yet.

You can ask AI:

> *"This word is unreadable. Based on the sentence, what are three likely words that could fit here?"*

You can also compare the structure of similar documents from the same time and place to reconstruct what *should* be there.

If a section is missing, ask AI what would typically appear in that part of the record during that era.

Sometimes the gap isn't a word — it's a date, a relationship, or a location. AI can help you narrow down the possibilities by analyzing patterns.

You can even upload a similar document from the same clerk or region to identify layout or phrasing habits that might guide your interpretation.

In this work, we don't throw away broken records — we decode them.

HOW TO USE AI AS A TRANSCRIPTION ASSISTANT

Once you've extracted a rough transcription, **you can prompt AI like this:**

> "I found a 1900 census page that lists the following: 'Marryan Johnson, age 32, race: Colored, occupation: Washerwoman, born: GA.' Help me confirm the spelling and determine possible matches in other years."

Or:

> "Can you identify key data points from this transcription and suggest how I should search for this person in earlier records?"

DON'T LET ILLEGIBILITY STOP YOU

Some of the most powerful breakthroughs in my research came from documents I nearly threw away. What looked like smudges became surnames. And what seemed unreadable became the key to my next discovery.

AI won't always get it right — but sometimes, it gets close enough to open a door.

Transcription isn't just about clarity. It's about access.

And when you can access what others left behind, you begin to write the story that was once too faint to see.

Bonus Tip: Don't Trust the First Read

AI tools may miss or misread info the first time — especially if:

- The document has stains, folds, or poor contrast
- The handwriting is inconsistent
- The scan was low-resolution

Tip: Try re-uploading with improved contrast or crop one section at a time. Then ask AI:

"What additional details do you notice now that weren't captured earlier?"

You'll often catch a middle name, a location, or a relative that was skipped the first time.

Use the worksheet sample sheet in **[Figure 8]** to track your uploads and what AI pulls from them. This helps you evaluate accuracy, stay organized, and know which records may need a second look.

Jot down important notes from this chapter:

✳ Figure 8: TRANSCRIPTION TRACKING SHEET

RECORD TYPE	TOOL USED	% CLARITY	EXTRACTED DATA

Figure 8: Transcription Tracking Sheet — AI-Assisted Document Log. Log the source, track which parts were unclear or corrected, and document any reclassification terms or unusual phrasing. It's designed to preserve accuracy while honoring the integrity of historical records.

CHAPTER 6

Six

Show Me the Source — Using AI to Find, Verify, and Cite Genealogy Records with Confidence

At some point in your genealogy journey, you'll find yourself staring at a name, a date, or a photo... and asking:

"Where did this come from?"

In the world of ancestry, it's not enough to know what — you need to know **where** it came from, **who recorded it**, and **how reliable** that source truly is. This chapter is about helping you ask the questions real researchers ask: *Is this accurate? Who said it? Can I prove it?*

With the help of AI, you can not only find the source — you can **trace it, verify it, and cite it** like a seasoned genealogist.

UNDERSTANDING THE TYPES OF SOURCES

Before you start tracing sources, you have to know what kind of document you're dealing with. Some records were created right in the moment — others were written years later by someone who only heard the story. And in between those two are copies, summaries, or interpretations that might leave out critical details. Knowing the difference helps you decide how much weight to give each one — and how to spot missing pieces.

A primary source carries the power of presence — it was recorded when the event happened, by someone who was there. A secondary source might still hold truth, but it's shaped by memory, perspective, and sometimes hearsay. A derivative source? That one's even further removed — and often reshaped by the hands of someone trying to summarize, not preserve.

This matters, especially for Black genealogy, where records were often filtered through people who didn't value the life they were documenting. A death certificate created the day someone passed is not the same as a biography written 50 years later — even if both are technically "sources." That distinction will shape how you prompt AI and how much trust you place in what you're reading.

Using AI, you can upload any of these and ask:

"Is this a primary or secondary source? What clues in the text support your answer?"

"Was this record likely written by a witness or someone retelling the event?"

Before You Use AI — Ask Yourself:

- Was this record created **at the time** of the event or **years later**?

- Who wrote this — **a direct witness**, **a relative**, or **an outsider**?

- Does this document **look original**, or does it **seem like a copy**?

- Are there **missing pieces** or **summarized parts** that might need more verification?

- Is there handwriting or formatting that suggests it was copied from another source?

- Does the tone feel clinical, emotional, or distant — and what does that tell me about the writer?

- Was this created by a government, a church, a family member, or a third party?

The better you understand the source, the better you can guide AI to read between the lines.

Every record type has its own language, structure, and purpose — and knowing what to expect helps you ask smarter questions. Let's take a look at common source types and examples in **[Figure 9]**.

SOURCE TYPES AND EXAMPLES

SOURCE TYPE	DEFINITION	EXAMPLE
PRIMARY	Created at the time of the event	Birth certificate, census, land deed
SECONDARY	Written after the fact	Obituary, biography, oral history
DERIVATIVE	A copy, transcript, or summary	Typed census extract. FindAGrave post

Figure 9: Source Types and Examples — Understand the difference between primary, secondary, and derivative sources so you can trace your research with clarity and confidence. Each type offers a piece of the truth — your job is to know how to read it.

Example: A birth certificate is a primary source, but an obituary written decades later may contain errors or secondhand memories — that's why knowing the source type matters.

USING AI TO TRACE THE ORIGINAL SOURCE

Let's say you find a name in someone else's family tree — but there's no citation. Before you adopt it, **you can ask AI:**

> "Can you search for records that confirm the birth of Henry Noble in Mississippi around 1880? Look for census, birth, or land records."

Or upload a screenshot and say:

> "Does this record look like it was copied from another tree or database? Can you help identify the original archive or collection?"

AI can help reverse-engineer where a record came from — especially when it's pulled from large ancestry databases without proper links.

CROSS-CHECKING CONFLICTING RECORDS

What happens when one document says 1879 and another says 1881? Or when a woman is listed as a daughter in one census and a niece in another?

This is where cross-referencing becomes essential. Don't rely on one document to tell the full truth — let AI help you compare sources, track patterns, and surface the most consistent storyline.

Prompt example:

> *"Compare the birth years for Lula M. Reed across these four records. Which is the most consistent, and why might the others differ?"*
>
> *Do any of these conflicting death dates seem more reliable based on the source type and proximity to the event?"*

AI will break down the differences for you — and even suggest which is likely to be most accurate based on internal consistency and context. But don't just take its answer at face value. Always weigh the record's origin, date, and purpose. A birth certificate written by a midwife in 1879 holds more weight than a delayed affidavit signed in 1942. And sometimes, the conflict reveals more than the correction — like remarriages, unofficial adoptions, or relatives covering up the truth.

See **[Figure 10]** below for comparison.

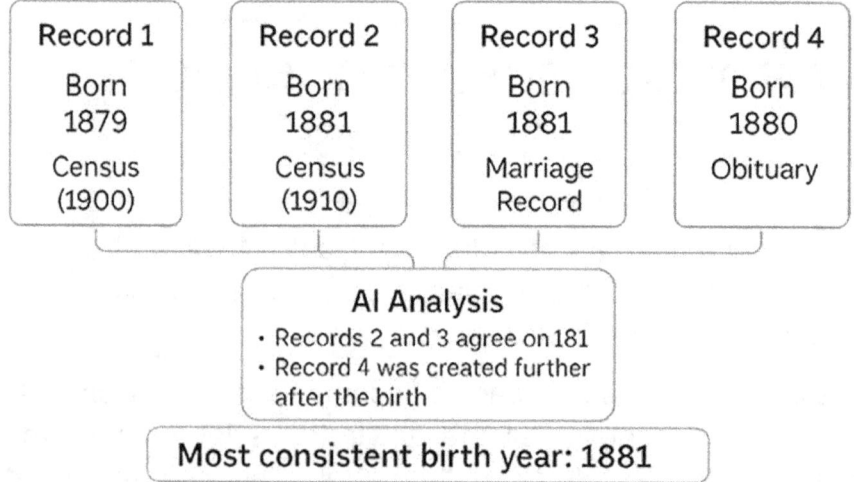

LET AI WRITE THE FOOTNOTE

Once you've verified a source, you want to **cite it clearly** — especially if you plan to share your findings, build a public tree, or write your own genealogy book.

You can simply say:

> "Please create a full source citation for this 1910 census entry, using Chicago or MLA style."

Or:

> "Can you create a simplified source note I can use under a photo in my genealogy binder?"

AI will generate both formal and informal citations, depending on your use.

REAL-LIFE USE CASE

When I uploaded a land record with no clear year, I asked AI to help me date it. AI compared the legal terms used in the document to known historical formats and narrowed it to a 5-year range — then confirmed it with a matching probate document from the same county.

I didn't just get the record. I got **clarity**.

AI didn't just provide an answer — it gave me a framework for how to approach similar cases in the future.

This is what AI brings to genealogy: not just tools, but a deeper understanding of how records interact with each other.

PROMPTS TO USE IN THIS PHASE

Before you trust any record, slow down and investigate its origins. Not every document is what it first appears to be — and understanding its creation story is just as important as the facts it holds. AI can help you cross-examine a record's background, but you must know what to ask. The right questions open doors that lazy research leaves shut. Every prompt you use in this phase strengthens the foundation you're building.

Ask questions that reveal the record's purpose, not just its content.

> *"What collection or archive might this record originate from?"*
>
> *"Is this document a copy or the original? How can you tell?"*
>
> *"Help me cite this record in formal genealogy format."*
>
> *"What makes this record a primary source versus a derivative?"*
>
> *"Are there other documents that would have been created at the same time as this one?"*
>
> *"Who was the intended audience for this record —*

and how might that affect what was included or left out?"

"What's missing from this record that would normally be expected?"

When you ask, *"Show me the source,"* you're doing more than double-checking facts — you're protecting the legacy. Every name, date, and document deserves to be **anchored in truth**. It's not about being perfect. It's about being *accountable* to the people you're honoring.

And when the paper trail fades or fails, your ability to prompt, verify, and cite with wisdom ensures that your family's story stands strong.

You are not just a tree builder. You are the **keeper of the evidence.**

Before you add any document to your tree, pause and ask: *Where did this come from, and how do I know it's accurate?*

Source verification is one of the most overlooked steps in genealogy — and one of the most crucial. **The Source Tracker Worksheet** in **[Figure 11]** helps you log what kind of record you're working with, where it came from, and how confident you are in its reliability.

When records don't agree, the **Conflicting Records Worksheet [Figure 12]** on the following page helps you compare discrepancies across sources and document your reasoning. Because building a legacy requires more than curiosity — it requires accountability.

🟢 Figure 11: SOURCE TRACKER CONFIRMING AND CITING GENEALOGY RECORDS

SOURCE	TYPE/VERIFICATION	CITATION
	Primary Secondary Derivative	
	Verification	
	CITATION	
	NOTES	

Figure 11: Source Tracker — Confirming and Citing with Confidence. This worksheet helps you document key details about the records you find, identify whether they're primary, secondary, or derivative sources, and assess how trustworthy each one is.

Getting Started: Using AI to Find Genealogy Records

❇ Figure 12: CONFLICTING RECORDS WORKSHEET

Ancestor:_____

Record	Details

Notes:
_____
_____

Possible Reasons for Conflicts:
_____
_____
_____

Figure 12: Conflicting Records Worksheet Tracking - Discrepancies Across Time. This worksheet helps you log conflicting details from multiple sources, compare their credibility, and document your reasoning behind which record you trust most. It's your tool for clarity when the paper trail doesn't line up.

Your ancestor might not show up by name — but the people around them will. Use AI to analyze neighbors, occupations, and addresses across time to confirm connections and uncover overlooked relatives.

AI Prompt: "What nearby individuals appear in multiple records with this person, and do their details help confirm family or community ties?"

CHAPTER 7

Seven

Searching Smart — Using AI to Find the Right Records

Once you've built a strong foundation and written your first few prompts, the next step is knowing where to direct your focus. Genealogy isn't about typing random names into a database and hoping for a miracle. It's about being strategic — understanding which records hold the deepest value, why they matter, and how to uncover them with clarity and confidence.

For Black American genealogy in particular, this step is critical.

So many of our stories have been buried, mislabeled, or scattered across fragmented records. AI can help you connect the dots — but only if you know where to look.

This chapter is your guide to that search. We'll walk through the records that tend to matter most in Black ancestry research, show you how to instruct AI to find them, and give you real-world strategies for making those discoveries count. Because when you search with intention, you don't just find documents — you find legacy.

WHICH RECORDS MATTER MOST — AND WHY

Not all records carry the same weight. For Black American families, certain types of documents are more likely to hold valuable information — not just because of what they say, but because of what they *reveal* when placed in the right historical and cultural context. Whether you're tracing formerly reclassified relatives, verifying oral history, or trying to confirm a migration path, some documents show up again and again as key puzzle pieces.

This section will guide you through *where* to focus your search — and how to instruct AI to help you uncover, decode, and connect these records with confidence.

1. **Census Records (especially 1870–1940)**

- 1870 is the first census that named formerly enslaved individuals.

- Use AI to track name changes and household patterns across decades.

Ask Artificial Intelligence to help build timelines and point out inconsistencies in relationships, birthplace, or age.

2. **Death Certificates**

    - Often contain maiden names, parent names, and informants who may be relatives.

    Use AI to extract details and connect informants to broader family trees.

3. **Marriage and Divorce Records**

    - Can link two family branches or reveal surname changes.

    Ask AI to generate a list of potential marriage record matches based on known surnames, dates, and counties.

4. **Freedmen's Bureau & Freedman's Bank Records**

    - Critical for the Reconstruction Era.

    Ask AI to cross-reference these with census data to identify patterns or missing relatives.

5. **Land Records & Deeds**

    - May indicate ownership, transfers within families, or connections to tribal land.

    Use AI to help you draft a property history or compare names in deed chains.

Military Records

- Great for locating men in the family, especially Civil War and WWI registrants.

Ask AI to help match draft cards with census data.

6. **Church and School Records**

- Local churches often kept baptism, funeral, and membership records.

Ask AI to assist in summarizing or transcribing these handwritten entries.

HOW TO GUIDE AI TOWARD THESE RECORDS

AI doesn't know the emotional weight behind your search — it just knows patterns. That's why *how* you ask is just as important as *what* you ask. When you're searching for records tied to Black American lineages, you're often working with names that changed, dates that shifted, and identities that were reclassified. So, the more context you give, the more helpful AI becomes.

You'll get better results if you tell AI what you're looking for — and *why* it matters. Let it know the person, the time period, the place, and the relationship. Don't just ask it to find someone. Tell it who they were to you, where they might have lived, and what legacy they left behind.

Here's a sample prompt:

"I'm looking for a death certificate for a Black woman named Emma Thomas, born around 1885 in Arkansas. Her husband was Henry Thomas. They lived in Jefferson County. Can you help me identify likely record matches or extract important names and relationships from a document image?"

By stating the *record type,* the *person*, the *location*, and your *goal*, you're giving AI the context it needs to be effective.

HOW AI HELPS DECODE CONFUSING RECORDS

This section will guide you through where to focus your search — and how to instruct AI to help you uncover, decode, and connect records with clarity and strategy. Because sometimes, the record you need isn't lost — it's just hard to read, mislabeled, or misinterpreted.

AI isn't just for finding new documents. It shines when it helps you make sense of the ones already in your hands — the blurry census scans, the overlapping dates, the mysterious household members listed with no clear connection. These are the moments where confusion sets in — and where AI, when guided correctly, can help bring the story into focus.

With the right prompts, you can ask AI to compare, clarify, and even suggest what might be missing. You'll learn how to turn confusion into clarity — one detail, one record, one revelation at a time.

> "Can you help clarify household relationships and identify potential errors or inconsistencies?"

Or, if you have multiple records with similar names, you can ask AI to compare them side by side. It can highlight name variations, mismatched birthdates, and possible connections you may have overlooked.

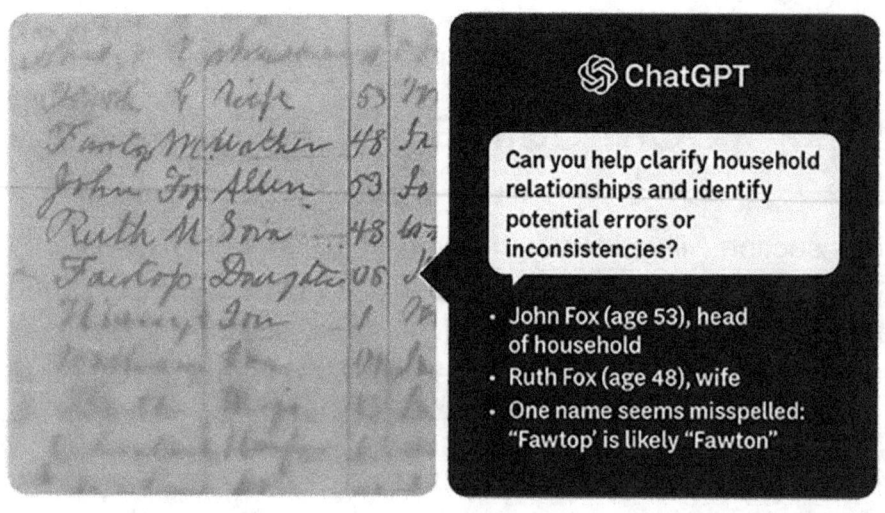

Not all records carry the same weight. For Black American families, certain types of documents are more likely to hold valuable information — not just because of what they say, but because of what they *reveal* when viewed through the lens of our history. A census may hold the name, but a death certificate might hold the mother. A Freedmen's Bureau record might seem dry, until you realize the labor terms echo a deeper truth.

Whether you're tracing formerly reclassified relatives, verifying oral history, or confirming a migration path, some documents show up again and again as key puzzle pieces in our ancestral legacy. Each one holds a fragment of truth that, when placed correctly, can transform your understanding of the entire tree.

Searching with AI isn't just about typing in a name. It's about asking the right question in the right way — and matching that question to the right record type.

The grid [see **Figure 13**] helps you to think like a strategic researcher, showing how to pair common genealogy questions with AI-driven prompts and the records most likely to hold answers.

AI SEARCH STRATEGY GRID

GENEALOGY QUESTION	RECORD TYPE	AI PROMPT EXAMPLE	FOLLOW-UP ACTION
Who were Sam Easton's parents?	birth record	Find a birth record for Sam Easton, born in Mississippi in 1871.	Ask for birthplace or names of parents
When did Louisa Henson die?	death certificate	Search for Louisa Hetison's death certificate in Arkansas between 1810 and 1820.	Request a summary of key details
Where did Henry Morgan live in 1920?	census record	Locate Henry Morgan of Georgia in the 1920 U.S. Census and list matching households	Find additional censuses for this person
How were Mary and Lena Jones related?	marriage record	Look up a Mississippi marriage record for Mary Jones and Lena Jones before 1890	Ask for name of parents or spouses

Figure 13: AI Search Strategy Grid — Matching Questions with Records. This table offers a smart approach to AI-assisted genealogy research. It connects real-world ancestral questions with the appropriate records, sample AI prompts, and next-step actions — helping you move from curiosity to clarity with intention.

Your questions carry power — and when asked with purpose, they can unlock doors that once seemed sealed shut. Use this grid to sharpen your focus and remind yourself that you're not just searching randomly — you're tracking legacy. Let each row be a reminder that records are not just data points; they're evidence of life lived, choices made, and stories waiting to be seen. And the more strategic you are with your questions, the clearer the answers will become.

BEWARE OF MISINFORMATION

Even AI can make incorrect assumptions — especially when records are incomplete or based on biased data. Always cross-check what AI tells you. Use its output as a *starting point*, not the final answer.

Examples of things to double-check:

- Relationships that aren't backed by documentation
- Broad or incorrect location suggestions
- Mislabeling of race or tribal affiliation
- Inconsistent dates that don't align with known historical timelines
- Misinterpretations of handwritten text or abbreviations

If something feels off, trust your instincts and revisit the source.

Genealogy is part logic, part intuition — and both matter.

AI might get you close, but only your discernment can get it right.

Remember, historical records were created in a system that didn't always recognize our humanity — AI is still learning how to correct that.

Your job isn't just to read — it's to interpret through truth, not assumption.

LET AI HELP BUILD A SEARCH PLAN

Sometimes the next step isn't obvious — and that's okay. You don't have to figure it all out alone. AI can be more than a search engine; it can act like a strategy partner. When used intentionally, it can help you map your next move and refine your research path.

Ask AI:

> *"Based on what I know so far, what five record types should I search next to trace Mary Bell's maternal line?"*

Or, ask AI to:

> *"Create a research checklist based on Black genealogy in Georgia between 1865 and 1930."*

Let AI act like a genealogy coach — always responding, but only as good as the information you feed it.

Don't be afraid to revisit this step often — your search plan should evolve as new clues come to light.

And remember: a well-crafted question today can save you months of circling dead ends tomorrow — so ask boldly, and guide the tool with purpose.

BE STRATEGIC, NOT RANDOM

AI is not about searching harder — it's about searching smarter.

It's not about how many records you find, but how well you understand the ones you already have. Random searches waste time and energy. Strategic searches build legacies.

You are not just hunting for documents. You are assembling a story from fragments — reconstructing lives that were scattered across censuses, misnamed in death records, and hidden in margins. Every question you ask, every record you pull, every clue you chase should move you closer to the truth.

AI can help speed up the process, but only if you slow down and search with intention. Think like a storyteller. Move like a detective. Prompt like a builder. And remember: the goal isn't just information — it's revelation.

Don't just ask AI what it sees — ask it what's missing.

Don't just follow a surname — trace its variations, migrations, and silences. Look at what was recorded and ask why. Then ask who wasn't included — and why not.

Strategy means asking layered questions.

It means comparing timelines, naming patterns, locations, and events.

It means using your instincts to decide when a record lines up — and when it's trying to lead you off course.

Some records will raise more questions than answers. That's not failure — that's a clue. That's a sign to dig deeper, to cross-check, to call on memory and method at the same time. The goal is not speed — it's clarity.

You are not just gathering data points. You're reconstructing a lived experience. And that takes skill, patience, and reverence.

When you know what to ask, where to look, and how to apply the findings — that's when the story rises from the paper. That's when records become revelations.

Use the worksheet in **[Figure 14]** to apply what you've learned by mapping your own genealogy questions to specific record types and AI prompts. This isn't just about searching — it's about strategizing. Use it to plan your next research move with clarity and purpose.

Jot down important notes from this chapter:

_____

_____

_____

_____

_____

_____

✳ Figure 14: AI SEARCH STRATEGY GRID

Every ancestor leaves a trail — you just need the right tools to follow it. Use this grid to write out your own questions, choose the best records, and craft powerful AI prompts that move your search forward.

QUESTION	RECORD TYPE	TIME & LOCATION
Where were they in 1870?	Federal Census	Southern States in 1870

- **PROMPT:** *Search the 1870 Census for _____*

What did they do for a living?	Freedmen's Bureau	Virginia, 1867

- **PROMPT:** *Show me the Freedmen's record for _____*

How were they classified?	Federal Census	Georgia, 1920

- **PROMPT:** *Find the occupation of _____ in Georgia.*

Who owned their labor or land?	Slave Schedule or Deeds	Alabama, 1850s

- **PROMPT:** *Identify the owner of _____ in 1850s Alabama.*

Getting Started: Using AI to Find Genealogy Records

Now it's your turn to create your own AI search strategy. Use what you've learned from the previous examples. Fill in your own genealogy question, choose the right record type, add the time and location, then write a tailored prompt that you could give to AI.

Your Question:

_____

Record Type: _____

Time and Place: _____

- **PROMPT:** _____

Your Question:

_____

Record Type: _____

Time and Place: _____

- **PROMPT:** _____

Figure 14: AI Search Strategy Grid — Guided Planning Worksheet This worksheet guides you through the process of transforming vague ancestral questions into focused research prompts. With space to identify your question, match it with a record type, and create a smart AI prompt, it turns guesswork into guided discovery.

FEATURED AI TIP

Don't just scan the document — scan the story. AI can help you find the names, but only you can feel the silence between them.

Use every search as a conversation with the past — and listen for what wasn't written.

CHAPTER 8

Upload, Analyze, Organize — Using AI to Extract Key Details from Documents

---

There comes a moment in genealogy when your digital shoebox of documents—birth certificates, census records, obituaries, deeds—starts to overflow. You've gathered the evidence, but the pile is starting to feel like a puzzle with no picture on the box. That's where this chapter comes in.

It's time to teach the AI how to help you clean house, extract the gems, and sort through your findings with clarity and strategy.

In this chapter, we'll walk through how to upload your documents into AI tools, analyze the contents, and organize the information into categories that help you see the bigger picture. And just like every other tool in this guide, these techniques aren't hypothetical — I've used them myself to uncover facts that were hiding in plain sight.

STEP 1: UPLOAD WITH INTENTION — CHOOSING THE RIGHT FORMAT

Start with the most accessible digital files in your collection. These might be:

- JPEG scans of death certificates
- PDFs of marriage licenses
- Screenshots of handwritten census pages
- Word documents of family notes or interview transcripts

💡 **Tip:** *Make sure your image or PDF is clear, cropped, and easy to read. Rename files with short, simple titles (like 1930_Census_EllisonHousehold.pdf) and* **avoid using spaces or special characters** *(such as /, %, &, #) — this helps AI platforms read and process them more smoothly.*

Here's how I like to start the process:

1. Choose 3–5 documents from the same branch of the family.

2. Rename each file with a short, clear title like

   "1930_Census_EllisonHousehold" or
   "1955_Obituary_RobertJReed."

3. Upload into an AI tool that supports document analysis, such as ChatGPT (with image or file upload), Claude, or even Microsoft Copilot for PDFs.

Start small, but start with intention.

After you've organized your records and prepared them for analysis, you're not just feeding data into a tool — you're setting the stage for revelation.

AI can help uncover connections you may have overlooked, but it's your clarity, context, and curiosity that bring the story to life.

STEP 2: ASK AI TO EXTRACT WHAT YOU CAN'T SEE ALL AT ONCE

Once your file is uploaded, your job is to prompt the AI like a research assistant. **You might say:**

> *"Please read this death certificate and pull out the following:*
>
> *Full name, age, date of death, place of death, cause of death, informant's name, and burial location."*

Or for a census record, say:

> *"Can you list every person in this household, their age, race, relationship to the head of household, and place of birth?"*

What you're doing here is transforming raw images or text into clean, usable **data points**.

Real-Life Use Case:

I uploaded a Missouri death certificate for one of my maternal ancestors and asked AI to extract every name listed. It not only pulled the deceased and informant but also caught the undertaker's name — a surname that matched a previously unconnected cousin. That one overlooked name helped me connect two family lines I'd kept separate for months.

It was a reminder that sometimes the key to the puzzle is hiding in plain sight — all it takes is sharper eyes and the right tool.

STEP 3: ASK AI TO INTERPRET THE DATA, NOT JUST TRANSCRIBE IT

Once you've extracted the raw details, don't stop there. Ask AI to **analyze the data** for patterns or clues. For example:

> "Do you notice any inconsistencies in this household between the 1910 and 1920 census?"

> "What can be inferred from the burial location on this certificate?"

> "Can you explain the significance of the informant's surname matching the mother's maiden name?"

> "Are any of these neighbors repeated across different census years — and could they be relatives?"

> "Does this migration timeline align with any major historical events that might explain the move?"

These are the kinds of questions that lead to break throughs. AI can't replace your intuition — but it can speed up how fast you see the connections that matter.

You can also prompt AI to suggest what information might still be missing — and what additional records could help fill those gaps. Every time you move beyond transcription and ask AI to think like an analyst, you take your research one step closer to revelation.

STEP 4: ORGANIZE YOUR RESULTS FOR THE LONG GAME

Now that you've pulled information from multiple documents, you need to store it in a way that supports your long-term research. **You can ask AI to help you format it like this:**

"Can you create a chart of the data extracted from these three documents, grouped by year and family member?"

Or:

"Organize these death records by maternal lineage based on maiden names mentioned."

Use Google Sheets, Airtable, Notion, or even a printable chart you can keep in a research binder. You can even ask AI to help generate the chart structure or categorize each entry.

The goal is clarity — not just for you, but for anyone who picks up your research in the future.

Well-organized data saves you time, prevents repetition, and reveals connections that scattered notes often hide.

Think of this step as investing in your future breakthroughs.

You're not just tracking names — you're building an ancestral map that others can follow. And when your work is this organized, it becomes a legacy resource — not just for your research, but for future generations who will build on what you've uncovered.

WHY THIS MATTERS FOR BLACK AMERICAN RESEARCH

For many of us, the challenge isn't a lack of records — it's the **quality and condition** of those records. Handwriting is messy. Names are misspelled. Our ancestors were reclassified, misidentified, or written out entirely. That means we don't have the luxury of relying on clean data. We have to **pull the truth out of the mess**, and that's what this method is designed to do.

It's about sharpening your ability to detect patterns others overlook. Because when the system fails to name us, we learn how to recognize ourselves anyway.

We know that one name might carry five spellings.

That a "boarder" might be a brother.

That a wrong birth year might be the result of someone guessing — not lying.

That our people often showed up in someone else's household.

And that *we were always there* — even when the ink tried to erase us.

And with the right questions — and the right tools — we can bring those hidden truths back to light.

FROM RAW DATA TO REVELATION — DECODING, ORGANIZING, AND MAPPING YOUR FAMILY'S STORY

Before you can build timelines, trace migrations, or map connections, you need clarity. That clarity starts here — by taking your raw records and using AI to decode every hidden detail they contain. Don't be afraid to re-upload the same document with different questions. That's not overdoing it — that's research done right.

And when something finally clicks — when a forgotten name matches a familiar place, or a pattern emerges that ties two generations together — you'll be glad you took the time to upload, analyze, and organize with intention.

Let the records speak — and trust that you now have the tools to listen with clarity and care.

MY ADVICE: DON'T JUST READ YOUR RECORDS — DIALOGUE WITH THEM

The reason I love using AI at this stage of the research process is because it gives me a second pair of eyes — without the bias. It doesn't assume 'Black' means 'slave.' And it doesn't gloss over the informant — who may hold the key to a larger family connection. It doesn't skip the burial place because it's unfamiliar. It responds to the questions I ask with a fresh set of lenses — and when you're building Black American genealogies, that fresh lens is powerful.

Sample Prompt Starters:

"Compare the ages of these siblings across two census records and highlight any errors."

"Does this death certificate suggest a hospital or home death?"

"Can you group these five marriage records by county and decade?"

"What does the occupation listed tell us about the family's status in 1940?"

So don't just let the record talk at you — talk back. The more you engage, the more the hidden details begin to reveal themselves.

Now it's time to bring those findings into focus.

You've gathered names, dates, locations, and sources. But raw information isn't enough — you need to see the story unfold.

This is where the family timeline becomes your blueprint.

When you lay out each generation, patterns begin to emerge. You'll start to notice gaps, migrations, and milestones that help you piece together what really happened.

Use worksheets in **[Figure 15]** to map it out. Keep it flexible. As you find new records, you can return and refine it. This is your working map — not just of dates, but of legacy.

Figure 15: FILLABLE TIMELINE WORKSHEETS

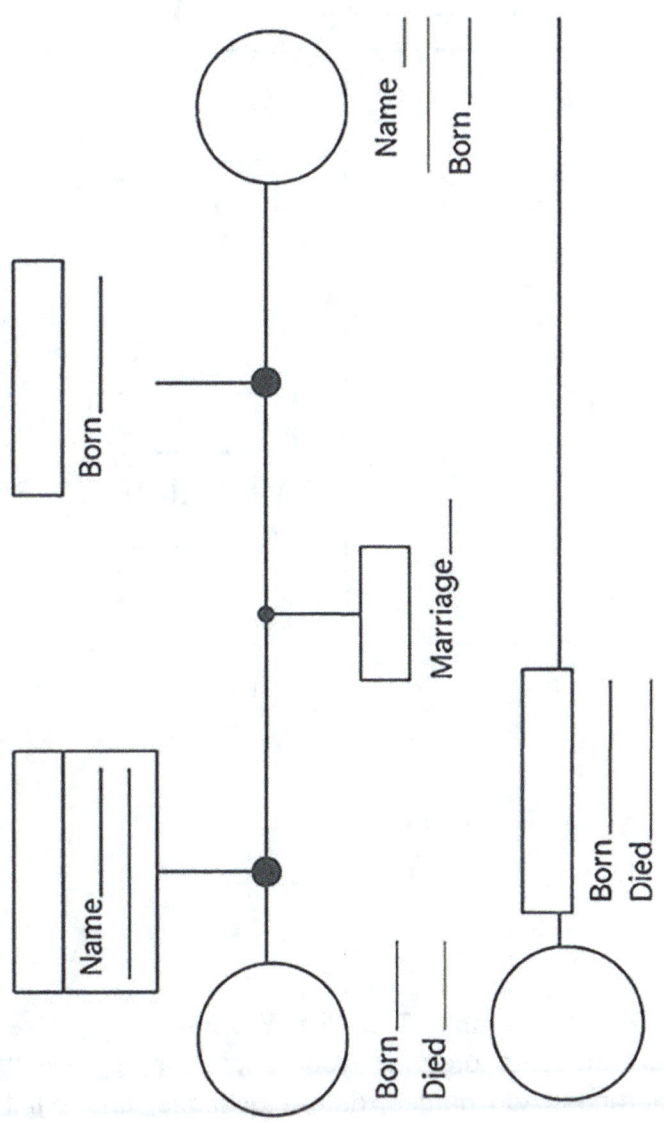

Rebuilding the Tree. A Black American Guide to AI Tools

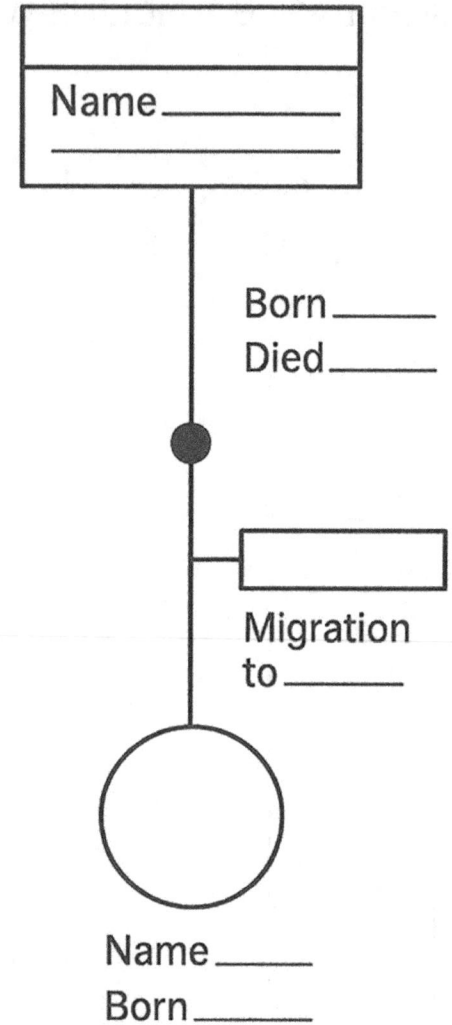

Figure 16: Fillable Timeline Worksheet — Use this visual guide to organize your ancestors' life events by generation. Add names, dates, locations, and significant moments to begin building a clearer family story.

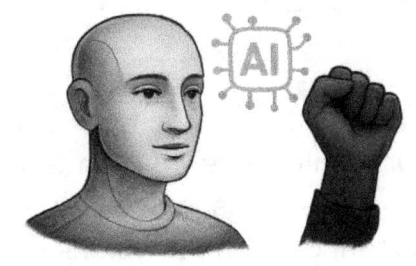

CHAPTER 9

Nine

The Power and the Pitfalls of AI in Black Genealogy

AI can do a lot — but it can't save you from assumptions, shortcuts, or misinformation. In fact, **it will follow your lead, even if that lead is based on flawed logic.** That's why it's important to slow down and examine the habits that may be sabotaging your research before AI ever enters the equation.

In the first half of this chapter, we'll cover the most common mistakes Black genealogy researchers make when working with AI — and how to avoid them.

MISTAKE #1: ASSUMING ALL BLACK AMERICANS CAME FROM AFRICA

This is one of the biggest missteps. If you start your search by assuming that your family came over on a slave ship, you've already eliminated entire lines of your tree that may have Indigenous, Caribbean, or even pre-colonial American roots.

When I first started searching for my own family, I asked AI about my ancestors "from Africa." But something didn't sit right. I couldn't find the ships. The stories didn't line up. Eventually, I had to reroute everything and begin searching as if my people were already *here*. That changed everything.

Correction: Be open to all possibilities. If you know your family was in Mississippi in the 1700s, start there. Don't let the algorithm steer you toward a false origin story.

MISTAKE #2: LETTING AI GUESS INSTEAD OF DIRECTING IT

AI will always try to be helpful. If you ask it, "Can you tell me about my ancestor Sarah Johnson?" without any other info, it will pull from the most common or available narratives — not your actual lineage.

Correction: Always include record types, locations, dates, and relationships. You are the driver. AI is just a vehicle.

MISTAKE #3: IGNORING RECLASSIFICATION PATTERNS

Black Americans were labeled as Negro, Colored, Indian, Mulatto, Servant — even White. These racial terms shifted by region, year, and census taker.

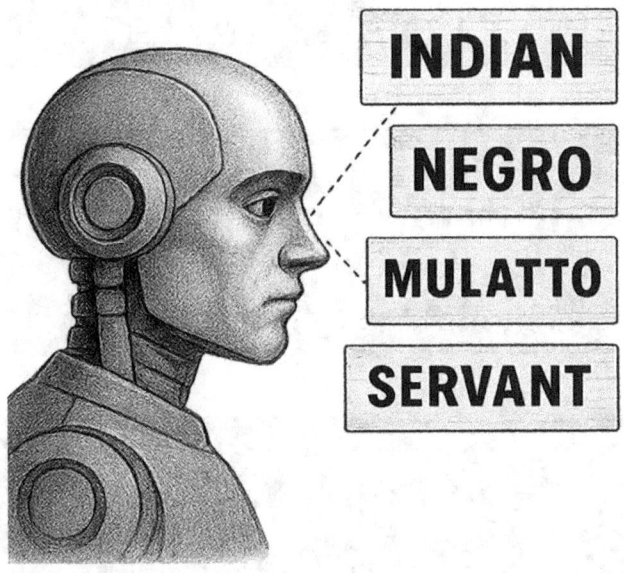

If you're only searching under "Black" or "African American," you're likely missing generations.

Correction: Tell AI to search for reclassification terms. I often include a prompt like:

> "This family may have been listed as Indian in 1880 and Negro by 1900. Include those variations."

Mistakes to Avoid

1 — **ASSUMING ALL BLACK AMERICANS CAME FROM AFRICA**
Correction. Be open to all possibilities.

⬇

2 — **LETTING AI GUESS INSTEAD OF DIRECTING IT**
Correction. Include dates, locations, relationships, and record types

⬇

3 — **IGNORING RECLASSIFICATION TERMS**
Black Americans were labeled as Indian in 1880 and Negro by 1900. Include those variations?

Correctionl Be sure to search for reclassification terms.

⬇

Correction. Be open to all possibilities.

MISTAKE #4: TAKING ARTIFICAL INTELLIGENCE AT ITS WORD

Let's be honest — we've all gotten excited over an AI-generated family story that sounded *too good to be true*. Sometimes, it *is*.

AI pulls from patterns, not personal knowledge. It doesn't know your Aunt Viola from anybody else's.

Correction: Always verify. Treat AI responses like leads, not facts. Go back to the records and confirm everything.

MISTAKE #5: USING SLAVE NARRATIVES AND PLANTATION RECORDS AS THE ONLY SOURCE

While these documents can be useful, they often reflect the lens of the enslaver — not the lived experience of your people. Too many researchers stop at what the plantation records say, never realizing those records were written to count property, not to honor legacy.

In my own journey, I once found an ancestor listed in a slaveholder's ledger as nothing more than "boy, strong arms." But it was a church ledger — tucked in a Black congregation's archive — that revealed his full name, his role as a deacon, and his children's names listed in a Sunday school roll. That changed everything.

Correction: Balance your sources. Use community records, oral histories, Freedmen's Bureau files, and Black church rosters to fill in the blanks. These are the places where your people left their truth — in their own way, on their own terms.

MISTAKE #6: NOT SAVING PROMPTS OR RESPONSES

If you're getting helpful results, but you're not saving your prompts, you'll end up recreating the wheel over and over again.

Correction: Keep a prompt log. I keep a dedicated journal where I write the best prompt structures that worked for me. This way, when I find a new record or lead, I can plug it into a proven format.

MISTAKE #7: RUSHING THE PROCESS

Legacy work takes time. You're building more than a tree — you're restoring memory."

AI may speed things up, but if you move too quickly, you'll skip over foundational details that give your tree depth and truth.

Correction: Take your time. Let every name lead you to a deeper question. Document your steps so the story isn't just fast — it's **accurate**. A quick tree is usually a shallow one.

Every document you skip might be the one that held the truth you needed.

This is legacy work — and legacy deserves patience.

RESPECT THE PROCESS

AI is a powerful tool, but it's only as good as the hands that guide it. Don't use it to shortcut your research — use it to support your diligence.

This journey is sacred. You're not just filling in names. You're **restoring memories**. And that kind of work deserves your **patience, discernment, and care**.

Treat every clue like it was left behind on purpose.

Slow down long enough to *listen* to the records — not just read them.

Understand that missteps will happen, but growth is part of the reward.

Don't rush revelation — honor it.

Because you're not just building a family tree…

You're rebuilding a legacy that was never supposed to survive — and doing it anyway.

Every ancestor you document adds a layer of truth to the record.

Honor the process by moving with clarity, not speed.

The more deliberate you are, the stronger and more reliable your tree becomes.

BEYOND THE MISTAKES: THE POWER & THE PITFALLS

Before we trusted these tools, we had to first ask:

1. *Whose data built the system?*

2. *Whose story got erased before the machine even started learning?*

AI is powerful — no doubt. It can read handwriting we can't, extract patterns across generations, and help us see what was hidden. But when it comes to Black genealogy, the very thing that makes AI useful also makes it dangerous.

It was trained on archives that often excluded us. It learned from datasets that labeled us as property, "mulatto," or "unknown." And unless we bring our discernment to the table, it can replicate the very systems we're trying to break.

In the second half of this chapter, we explore the dual reality:

✊🏾 The power of AI to speed up and deepen ancestral research

🚨 The pitfalls of AI rooted in bias, erasure, and lazy assumptions

Because before you use the tool, you've got to know how it was trained — and more importantly, how to retrain it to serve your mission.

WHAT AI MAKES POSSIBLE FOR BLACK RESEARCHERS

AI can do things in minutes that once took days — or generations. What used to require long nights at the courthouse or weeks waiting on microfilm now happens in seconds — right at your fingertips. And while it may not replace your intuition or lived experience, it can amplify what you already know. This is about working smarter, not surrendering the sacred.

🔍 Transcribe messy records faster than human eyes

📇 Write profiles, stories, and reports in your tone

🧠 Find pattern matches between surnames, dates, and places

📁 Organize documents into timelines, summaries, and searchable formats

🔑 Cross-reference clues from multiple sources to create a bigger picture

AI helps you work like a one-person archive team — if you use it with clarity and purpose. It's not just about speed — it's about expansion. The more you teach it what matters to your people, the more powerful your results become.

I've had AI catch a name pattern I almost missed, or pull a land record I didn't think to search. It can even reveal migration patterns when you line up census records by state and decade. It's the kind of tool that doesn't just support your research — it strengthens your strategy.

The key is staying in the driver's seat — you guide the mission, AI carries the load.

WHAT AI DOESN'T UNDERSTAND (UNLESS YOU TEACH IT)

Even the most advanced system can fail your family if it was trained on narrow-minded perspectives, flawed assumptions, or archives that were never meant to preserve your truth.

AI is only as accurate as the lens it was built through — and for Black American genealogy, that lens has been historically distorted. It can misread, mislabel, or completely miss what matters most.

🏛 Biased archives created to erase "Black Indigenous American contributions

📃 Records that misclassified your ancestors and rewrote their origin

👹 Language that defaults to "enslaved" when seeing "Negro," even post-Emancipation

🌍 Assumptions that all Black Americans came from Africa

That's why prompting with clarity and cultural context is non-

negotiable. AI can only reflect the data it was trained on —
and much of that data was never made with your ancestors in
mind.

⚠ REAL-WORLD EXAMPLES OF PITFALLS

These aren't just hypotheticals — they're real examples of how AI can go wrong when it's fed biased, incomplete, or misinterpreted data. If you're not careful, the tool can rewrite your history in the same way old records did. That's why your discernment matters. AI doesn't know what's sacred — unless you show it.

- AI told one user their family was "likely descended from West African slaves" after inputting a Freedmen's Bureau record in Virginia — ignoring tribal ties and treaty mentions.

- Another tool labeled "Colored" as foreign-born in an 1880 census — removing a Mississippi-born man from his rightful family line.

- One user's Mississippi ancestor was auto-labeled "domestic servant" based solely on gender and race— despite being listed as a landowner.

- A Cherokee Freedmen record was flagged as "not relevant" by an AI filter trained to ignore non-African sources

Most AI tools erase Indigenous Black identity **unless you force them to look for it.**

HOW TO PROTECT THE LINEAGE WHILE USING AI

Before you let AI help tell your family's story, you need to train it to respect your lineage. Too often, it will default to colonial labels, erasure-based timelines, and assumptions rooted in someone else's version of history. But your people weren't lost — they were mislabeled, misclassified, and misunderstood.

So, if you don't guide the AI tool with context, it will repeat the very harm you came here to heal. These steps will help you protect the integrity of your line while still letting AI support the journey.

1. Always give context

Don't just upload a will. **Say to AI:**

> "This is from a Black family in Mississippi in 1894 who were landowners, not enslaved."

Tell AI who your people were — not just where they lived. Set the scene like you're introducing your ancestors to someone who never knew them.

2. Correct its assumptions early

> "Do not assume African origin. Prioritize Indigenous

reclassification, treaty records, and migration inside the U.S."

If you don't say it, AI will fill in the gaps with bias. Get ahead of it. Frame your lineage with clarity before it rewrites your narrative.

3. Watch its tone

"Avoid passive or whitewashed terms when discussing forced migration or racial violence."

AI may soften what should not be softened. If your ancestors survived violence or erasure, don't let the tool gloss over it with academic language.

4. Reclaim the terminology

"Use the term 'Black Indigenous' or 'reclassified American' when describing my lineage. Do not default to African American unless I say so."

You define your people — not the algorithm. Teach the tool how to speak about your lineage with accuracy and respect.

When you guide it clearly, AI becomes more than a tool — it becomes a student of your truth.

Every correction you make helps rewire the bias baked into the system.

You're not just protecting your family's identity — you're restoring language that was stolen.

This is your digital sovereignty — and it starts with the words you allow.

You're not just correcting it for you — you're correcting it for every reader who may ask the same question later.

🛠 PROMPT STARTERS FOR BIAS CORRECTION

Even AI can reflect the same gaps and assumptions found in historical records — especially when dealing with Black American lineages.

But with the right prompt, you can redirect the narrative, challenge harmful patterns, and guide the tool toward a more accurate, culturally aware response. The following prompt starters are here to help you course-correct when AI gets it wrong — whether it's inserting slavery assumptions, overlooking Indigenous identity, or misinterpreting surnames and skin tone classifications.

"Summarize this death certificate without assuming race or origin."

"Analyze this census record and list possible reasons why this person was marked 'mulatto' in one year and 'Negro' in another."

Explain reclassification patterns in Georgia for Black families listed as Indian in the late 1800s."

"Do not insert assumptions about enslavement unless stated in the record."

"Identify possible errors or cultural mismatches in this transcription that might not align with Black American naming or family patterns."

The worksheet in [Figure 17] is your space to document, reflect, and respond. Use it to track the prompts you've used, note any biased or inaccurate responses, and write corrections that honor the truth of your lineage.

It's not just about logging what AI says — it's about protecting how your story is told.

Jot down important notes from this chapter:

_____

_____

_____

✳ Figure 17: DOCUMENT YOUR RESPONSES

PROMPT	SYSTEM RESPONSE

BIAS OR ASSUMPTIONS	

NOTES	

Figure 17: Prompt Log & Bias Correction Worksheet — Protecting Your Lineage While Using AI

Part II
Mastering The Prompts

If the ancestor you're searching for isn't showing up, follow the ones who knew them.

Prompt AI: "Act as a genealogy assistant. Help me find records for [Your Ancestor's Name] by searching for known relatives like [Sibling Name], [Cousin Name], or neighbors listed on nearby census pages in [Location] between [Year Range]."

CHAPTER 10

Your First Prompt — Talking to AI Like a Research Assistant

AI is not magic — it's mimicry. It takes the input you give it and mirrors back what it calculates to be most useful based on the structure of your request. So, in genealogy research, the way you ask matters.

You don't need to be technical or speak in code. But you do need to be clear, specific, and informed. This chapter will teach you how to write a genealogy prompt that gets AI working for you — not against you.

When your question is vague, AI wanders. When your prompt is focused, AI follows your lead.

THINK OF AI AS YOUR RESEARCH ASSISTANT — NOT THE EXPERT

AI is here to help process, organize, compare, and summarize. But it doesn't know your family. It doesn't know your tone, your culture, or the context of Black American reclassification.

That's your job to provide.

Here's the mindset shift: *You're the lead researcher. AI is the intern.* It's powerful and fast, but **it needs training**. If you give vague or broad prompts, you'll get generic results.

So before typing anything in, ask yourself:

- What do I already know about this person, record, or event?
- What *exactly* am I trying to uncover or verify?
- What names, locations, or dates do I have?

Be specific about what you want. Don't just say "help me with my family tree" — say who, where, and when.

Use full names and known relationships. Include details like "my great-grandfather, born around 1880 in Mississippi."

Mention the document type or clue you're working from. Census, death certificate, obituary, land deed? Tell AI what you're looking at.

Set boundaries for the search. Limit by decade, location, or relationship so AI doesn't go off track. Then, structure your prompt accordingly.

THE ANATOMY OF A GOOD GENEALOGY PROMPT

YOUR FIRST PROMPT
— Talking to AI Like a Research Assistant

When it comes to getting results from AI, the *quality of your question* is everything. A weak prompt leaves AI guessing, and you'll end up with generic fluff or irrelevant facts.

But a well-structured genealogy prompt?

That's like handing your assistant a roadmap and a flashlight. In this chapter, we'll break down what makes a strong prompt — so instead of wandering in circles, AI can help you dig deeper, faster, and with purpose.

Here's a weak prompt:

> *"Can you tell me about my grandfather James Reed?"*

This will give you a wide, unhelpful response. AI has no context.

Now let's improve it:

> *"I'm researching my maternal grandfather, James Reed, born around 1898 in Mississippi. He later moved to St. Louis, Missouri. His wife's name was Lillian, and their first child was born in 1922. I'm trying to locate him in the 1920 or 1930 census. Can you help me create a timeline or identify possible records?"*

Notice what you included:

- ✓ Relationship (maternal grandfather)
- ✓ Approximate birth year
- ✓ Birth and migration location
- ✓ Spouse and child's name
- ✓ Specific record types

Once you've organized your information, you can structure your actual AI prompt to sound more like this:

"Act as a genealogy researcher. Help me find records for my grandfather, James Reed, who was born around 1895 in Mississippi and later lived in St. Louis, Missouri. He may have worked for the railroad. I'm looking for census records between 1900 and 1940."

Now AI has context, location, dates, and a goal — and you've just turned a guess into a guided search.

> Can you tell me about my grandfather James Reed?

Her's a strong version of that same prompt:

> Act as a genealogy researcher. Help me find records for my grandfather, James Reed, who was born around 1895 in Mississippi and later lived in St. Louis, Missouri. He may have worked for the railroad. I'm looking for census records between 1900 and 1940.

With this detail, AI can build context, recognize surnames, and help you identify patterns — or even offer alternate spellings and variations.

It starts to trace *like* an elder — slow at first, but deep.

That's when the hidden branches in your family line start showing up.

INCLUDE CULTURAL CONTEXT IN YOUR PROMPT

This part is critical for Black American research — and it's often what makes the difference between a dead end and a breakthrough. AI doesn't know what it means when an entire family disappears from the census for a decade. It doesn't understand how names were changed, downgraded, or erased based on race, status, or land ownership. It doesn't recognize that being listed as "Mulatto" in 1880 could mean they were once classified as "Indian" just twenty years before.

So that's where you come in.

You'll want to include notes like:

> "Records may be under the term 'Colored' or 'Mulatto'"

> "This family may have been reclassified from Indian to Negro"

> "This family may have changed counties to avoid racial reclassification or land disputes"

> "Surnames in this line may have tribal origin, not from slavery"

> *"This region had heavy Black Indian presence pre-1900s"*

Artifical Intelligence doesn't automatically consider racialized data or reclassification patterns — but *you can teach it to.* Adding these cues into your prompt **trains AI** to think more like a **culturally aware researcher**.

REFINING YOUR PROMPTS — TRIAL AND ERROR IS NORMAL

AI is powerful, but it's not psychic — it needs your clarity to deliver results.

Think of prompting like teaching: if the student doesn't understand, you don't give up — you rephrase.

The process of trial and error isn't a mistake; it's a method.

Let's say your first AI prompt didn't get you the results you expected. Don't quit — refine.

Break your prompt down into parts:

- Is my name or date range too vague?
- Did I forget to mention known family members?
- Did I specify the record type I'm looking for?

Use follow-up prompts like:

> "Based on that timeline, can you help me identify

nearby families with similar surnames in the 1910 census?"

Or:

"Can you help me compare the 1880 and 1900 census data for this county to identify migration trends for Black families?"

This is where AI starts becoming a partner, not just a tool.

QUICK PROMPT TEMPLATES

Prompts don't have to be complicated — they just have to be clear. The goal is to guide AI like a research assistant who's learning your rhythm and priorities. To help you get started faster, here are some examples you can reuse and adapt:

Timeline Generator

"Help me create a timeline for [Name], born around [Year] in [Place], married to [Spouse], first child born in [Year]. Possible surnames include [List]. I'm searching census and military records between [Year] and [Year]."

Census Tracker

"Can you locate [Name], a Black man born ~1875 in [Place], likely listed as Colored or Mulatto, living in [Second Location] by 1910? Check 1880–1930 census records."

Surname Variations

"Give me alternative spellings or regional variations for the surname [Name] used in the American South between 1850 and 1920 among Black or Indigenous families."

Record Finder

"I'm looking for death records, land deeds, or Freedmen's Bureau data for a Black woman named [Name], born around [Year], living in [County, State]. What archives or databases might hold this info?"

TALK TO AI LIKE IT'S SMART, BUT NOT ALL-KNOWING

The more **specific**, **respectful,** and **context-rich** your prompt, the more valuable the output. Don't worry about grammar or perfection. Just be thorough and intentional.

Because when you combine your ancestral insight with this tool, you're not just searching — you're restoring.

AI isn't a genie or a mind reader — it works with what *you* give it.

So if you feed it weak input, expect shallow answers. But if you approach it like a research assistant — with dates, names, context, and goals — it can reveal patterns you've overlooked.

Tell it what you're trying to prove, not just what you're trying to find.

If you think something is missing or misclassified, say that upfront. Artificial Intelligence doesn't replace your instinct — it sharpens it.

Now, let's write your first prompt.

✸ Figure 18: PROMPT FORMULA FLOWCHART

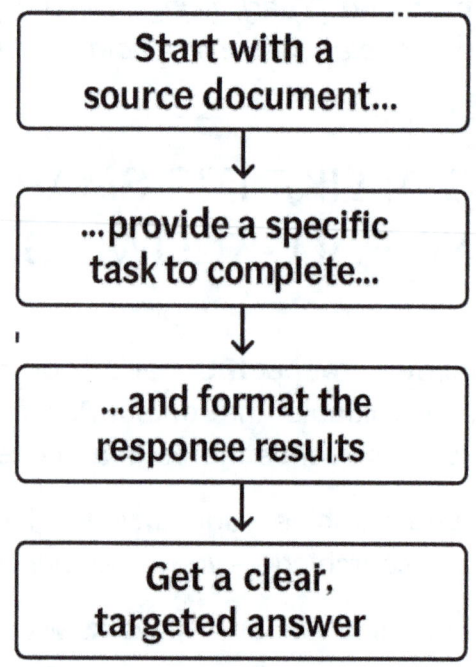

Figure %: Prompt Log Checklist

Now, use this space to build a strong, bias-aware AI prompt based on your own research document. Follow the same structure from the Prompt Formula Flowchart.

1. Start with a source document...

📝 *What document are you using?*

_____

2. Provide a specific task to complete...

📝 *What do you want AI to do with this document?*

_____

_____

3. Format the response results...

📝 *How should the results be organized or delivered?* (e.g., summary, chart, list)

_____

_____

4. Get a clear, targeted answer

📝 *Now write your full AI prompt below using all of the pieces above*

Prompt:

_____

_____

_____

FEATURED AI TIP

Sometimes your ancestor's name disappears — but the land doesn't.

AI can help trace the land instead: by location, acreage, neighbors, or deed transfers tied to a surname or region.

AI Prompt: "Can you find land records or deeds for this area and trace who owned or lived on it over time?"

CHAPTER 11

The Power of the Prompt — Asking Better Questions to Get Better Ancestral Answers

---

At the heart of every powerful discovery is a powerful question.

AI tools are only as strong as the prompt you give them — and when it comes to genealogy, the difference between *"What does this say?"* and *"What are the deeper clues in this* *record?"* can completely change your outcome. In this chapter, we'll break down how to **ask better questions**, fine-tune your language, and use AI like a real research partner — not just a digital assistant.

Because let's be honest — as Black Americans, we're not just searching for dates and names. We're recovering legacy. That requires layered thinking, sharp intuition, and the kind of prompts that cut through the confusion and get to the heart of the story.

WHY PROMPTS MATTER IN GENEALOGY

You could show the same document to five different researchers and get five different stories. Why? Because they're all **asking different questions.**

Your job isn't just to upload the record — *it's to interrogate it with intention.*

AI can't read between the lines unless you *ask it* to. And sometimes, the best prompts are the ones you didn't know you needed until you started digging.

One small detail — like a date, witness name, or signature — can shift your entire understanding.

Asking layered questions helps AI return more than surface answers.

Don't stop at "who" and "when" — ask "why here?" and "what

was happening around them?"

Prompting is how you move from names on paper to lives with context. This is how records become revelations.

START WITH THIS FORMULA: WHO + WHAT + WHY + WHEN

Before you type your next question into AI, take a moment to pause and get strategic. The most powerful prompts aren't the ones filled with fancy words — they're the ones rooted in clarity, intention, and structure. That's why this simple four-part formula — **WHO, WHAT, WHY, and WHEN** — can take your AI queries from surface-level to soul-deep.

This isn't just about asking a question. It's about guiding the

AI through the same mental process you'd go through when sitting with a confusing record or unraveling a family mystery. Think of it like opening a door to ancestral truth, one question at a time.

Let's break this down with a few examples:

- **WHO:** Is this person listed anywhere else in the record or nearby?
- **WHAT:** What roles or labels are being used (servant, boarder, widow)?
- **WHY:** Why might their name be spelled differently here?
- **WHEN:** Is this record consistent with others in that same time period?

Now combine them:

> "Compare the name Lula May Smith across three census records. Could changes in spelling and age suggest this is the same woman? Consider who else was in the household and what was happening in that decade".

This one prompt can give you *pages* of insight.

🧠 VISUAL TOOL:

See **[Figure 19]** for an example of a *Smart Prompt Builder* **chart** that breaks down how to combine **WHO, WHAT, WHY,** and **WHEN** into deeper, layered AI prompts. This is the strategy that shifts you from asking basic questions to unlocking powerful, generational answers.

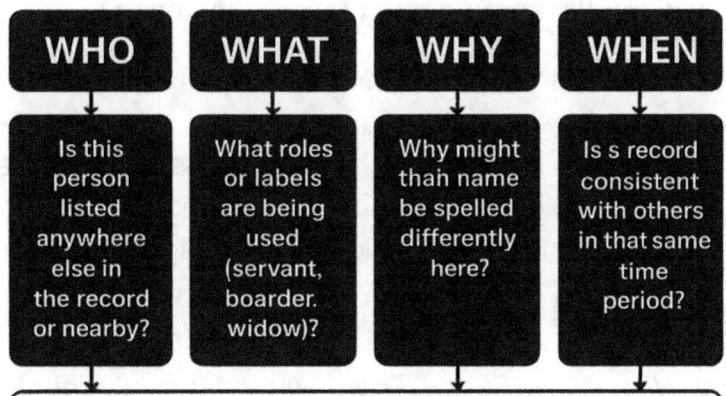

Figure 19: Smart Prompt Builder — Transforming Simple Questions Into Deep Genealogy Discoveries. This flowchart helps you build layered prompts by combining WHO, WHAT, WHY, and WHEN into a powerful research inquiry.

HOW TO TRAIN AI TO THINK LIKE A RESEARCHER

AI doesn't think — it calculates. But you can *guide* it to respond like a researcher by asking layered, thoughtful questions that build upon each other. This isn't about getting quick answers. It's about getting meaningful ones.

Think of it like teaching an intern how to analyze a complex case: you don't ask one big question and expect a perfect answer. You walk them through the process step by step — and that's exactly how you train AI. The more structure and direction you give, the more insightful the response will be.

Try using layered prompts like:

> "First, list all names. Then group by household. Finally, compare them to the prior decade's record and tell me what changed."

> "Give me a bullet-point summary, then tell me what might be missing based on the pattern of data."

> "Start by identifying all surnames in this document. Then cross-check for alternate spellings or phonetic variations in nearby counties."

> "Summarize what's consistent across each census year, then highlight any major shifts in age, race, or location."

The goal is to **stack your requests** so AI gives you more than just a surface-level answer — it gives you something you can build a story on.

PROMPT TYPES BY RECORD

Let's break it down by document type, so you can prompt smarter no matter what record you're looking at.

📜 Census Records

"Summarize the structure of this household and flag any inconsistencies in birth years."

"Compare this household in 1910 and 1920. Who moved in or out?"

"Are there any surnames repeated in nearby households?"

🏷️ Death Certificates

"List all names, relationships, and locations. Highlight informants or undertakers with matching surnames."

"What clues suggest family origin or migration patterns?"

"Could this burial location indicate tribal, religious, or family land?"

"Does the cause of death or attending physician

connect to other family members on nearby certificates?"

🏠 Land and Probate Records

"Translate this will into plain English and list heirs by generational order."

"Identify land parcels and who they passed to."

"Is this land still in the family or was it sold to outsiders?"

📷 Photos and Family Interviews

"Based on the clothing and background, what year could this photo be from?"

"Could this interview transcript contain surnames or locations worth researching?"

"Summarize what this oral history says about migration, occupation, or trauma."

THE PROMPT EVOLVES AS YOU GROW

When you first begin, your prompts will sound like:

"What does this say?"

"Who is in this household?"

"What year was this written?"

"Who signed this record?"

But as you grow, your questions evolve:

"What does the change in occupation tell us about this man's status?"

"Does the presence of a midwife instead of a doctor tell us anything about medical access?"

"What clues in this record suggest land ownership or displacement?"

You stop asking like a beginner… and start prompting like a **historian**.

REAL-LIFE PROMPT EXAMPLE

When I uploaded a Freedmen's Bureau labor contract to AI and asked,

"What does this document say?" — I got a short, generic summary:

"This is a labor agreement between a landowner and formerly enslaved workers outlining their wages and responsibilities."

But when I changed the question and asked:

"What power dynamics are at play in this labor contract?" — everything shifted.

AI began pulling details I hadn't even considered.

It flagged:

- The **unequal wage terms** between male and female laborers
- A clause about withholding payment for "disobedience" — language that echoed plantation discipline
- The use of **military-style oversight**, like the presence
- of guards and the restriction of movement
- And even the fact that the workers had **no legal representation**, while the landowner had the backing of federal agents
- The names of the witnesses — which included local officials who profited from the system
- The absence of dates that could signal contract renewals without consent
- The repeated use of vague terms like "hand" or "servant" that concealed real job roles
- And how the contract mimicked earlier Black Codes in its structure and enforcement

Suddenly, this wasn't just a contract. It was a **continuation of control**, cloaked in legality.

It was the post-slavery system finding a new way to bind Black labor — this time with signatures instead of Black labor— this time with signatures instead of chains. That one prompt didn't just help me interpret the document.

It changed how I **told the story of that ancestor**.

TRY THESE HIGH-POWERED PROMPTS TODAY

By now, you've learned how to structure a basic prompt, refine it, and layer your questions. But some records require more than logic — they require intuition. That's where these high-powered prompts come in. These are designed for when the trail goes cold, the clues get murky, or the deeper meaning is just out of reach.

These prompts are not just about getting data — they're about tapping into memory, context, and ancestral insight. When you ask these kinds of questions, you're not just using AI.

You're awakening the story beneath the silence.

"What deeper social or legal context might affect how this person was listed?"

"Could this occupation or location suggest tribal affiliation or ancestral land?"

"Are there clues that this person was reclassified between 1880 and 1900?"

"What might this nickname evolve from in formal records?"

"Does this record suggest someone else in the family was erased, omitted, or renamed?"

"What laws or policies were active in this region at the time — and how might they impact this record?"

"Compare this entry to others on the same page — what stands out or feels inconsistent?"

"What questions would a community elder ask if they saw this record today?"

Prompting isn't just typing — it's spiritual listening. It's asking the right question to unlock a buried memory. It's trusting your curiosity enough to press deeper, again and again.

AI will only give you what you're bold enough to ask for. So don't just ask "what." Ask **why.** Ask **who else.** Ask **what's missing.**

And when you do — you'll start seeing answers your ancestors have been waiting for someone to ask.

📝 **INTERACTIVE TOOL:**

Use the worksheet sample in **[Figure 20]** to craft your own layered AI prompt.

Start by identifying WHO, WHAT, WHY, and WHEN — then bring them together into one focused question to guide your ancestral research.

The more you practice asking clear, intentional questions, the more the answers will reveal themselves.

Your ancestors aren't lost — they're waiting for the right prompt to bring them back into the light.

Jot down important notes from this chapter:

_____

_____

_____

_____

_____

_____

❋ Figure 20: PROMPT BUILDING WORKSHEET: DEVELOPING ANCESTRY-FOCUSED QUESTIONS WITH AI

STEP 1. IDENTIFY

Fill in the WHO, WHAT, WHY, AND WHERE to gather key details.

1. Who is mentioned in the records?

WHO	

2. What happened, or what was documented?

WHAT	

3. Why is this record significant?

WHY	

4. When did this take place?

WHEN	

STEP 2. COMBINE

After gathering key details, bring them together into one focused question. Finally, write your AI Prompt:

PROMPT

Figure 20: Prompt Building Worksheet — This worksheet helps you break down complex genealogy questions into clear, layered prompts that AI can understand and respond meaningfully. By combining subject, context, intent, and time frame, you train AI to work more like a research partner.

The more clear and intentional your questions, the more insightful, relevant, and accurate AI's responses will be — because the quality of the answer always begins with the clarity of the prompt.

FEATURED AI TIP

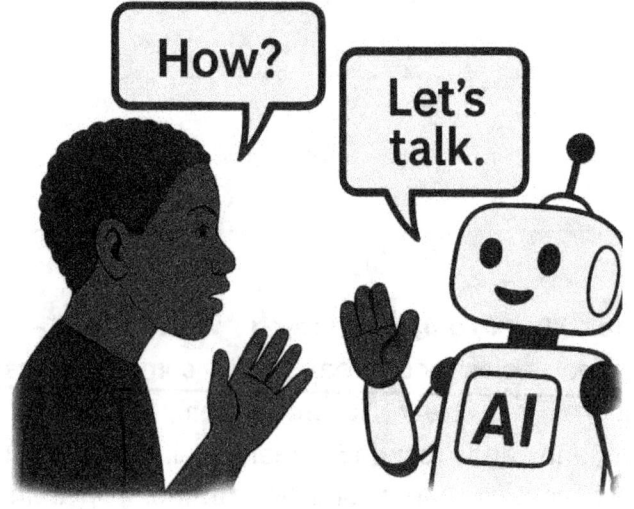

AI isn't magic — it mirrors your instruction. Train It Like a Student, Not a search bar Ask clear, layered questions. Teach it your lineage. Guide it with your tone. The more you explain, the more it remembers how to help *you*.

CHAPTER 12

Twelve

Guiding the Journey — Using AI to Create Research Plans and Next Steps

---

There comes a moment in every genealogist's journey when you stop chasing random records and start **moving with intention**. That's the shift — from scattered searching to strategic discovery. This chapter is about letting AI become your **research guide**, helping you track what you've found, what you're missing, and what your next best steps should be.

Because finding one ancestor is great. But uncovering the *whole story* requires direction.

WHY YOU NEED A RESEARCH PLAN

It happens to almost every researcher.

You start out with excitement — clicking through records, uncovering names, filling in branches. But before long, the trail gets muddy. You start chasing any record that "might" be connected, bouncing between generations, forgetting where you left off last time.

That's the moment when the thrill of discovery starts to feel more like digital quicksand.

That's where a research plan comes in. It doesn't just organize your thoughts — it gives your work direction. It helps you stop reacting and start leading the search. Because without a clear strategy, it's easy to:

- Get stuck following unrelated leads
- Overlook key people or records
- Forget where you've already searched
- Waste time repeating the same searches

A solid plan doesn't mean you know everything — it just means you know *what you're aiming to find next.*

And here's where AI becomes your personal research assistant.

It can help you build a step-by-step plan **[Figure 21]** based on your exact situation — not some generic checklist or beginner advice. Whether you're tracking a missing marriage record or trying to link two generations together, AI can help you map it out with precision.

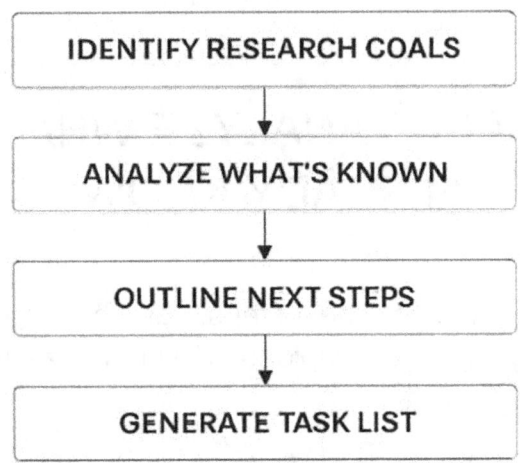

Figure 21: Building a Custom Research Plan with AI — Step-by-Step Flow

You don't need all the answers to move forward — just the right questions.

And when you ask them with intention, AI can help you uncover patterns you didn't even see yet.

It can lay out timelines, flag inconsistencies, and suggest what to look for next.

Not just *what's there* — but what's *missing*.

This is how you stop spinning your wheels and start building a strategy.

Genealogy is puzzle work.

AI helps you gather the edges — but *you* bring the picture into focus.

And now, you're ready to guide the search like a seasoned researcher.

USING AI TO ANALYZE WHAT YOU ALREADY KNOW

Before AI can guide your next steps, you need to show it what you've already gathered. Upload or summarize your current progress, like:

> *"I have census records for Lula May Reed from 1910, 1920, and 1940, but nothing before 1900."*

> *"I know my great-grandfather was born in Virginia, but I don't know when or where he migrated."*

Then ask:

> *"Based on this timeline, what documents should I search for next?"*

> *"Which relatives are missing key records like birth, marriage, or land ownership?"*

AI tools can scan for **gaps, inconsistencies, and opportunities**, helping you get laser-focused in your search.

Even if your notes feel scattered, AI can help you turn fragments into a foundation.

LET AI RECOMMEND NEXT STEPS — BASED ON LOGIC AND PATTERN

Once AI understands what you've already found, it can help you figure out what to do next — not randomly, but based on the logic hidden in your own research. Every missing record, date gap, or place change becomes a clue. And when you ask the right kind of question, AI can turn those clues into strategy.

Example prompts:

> *"What records are most likely to contain information about someone born in Tennessee in 1882 but missing from the 1900 census?"*

> *"Can you build a research strategy for finding Black landowners in Georgia between 1870–1920?"*

> *Or even:*

> *"Give me five steps to break through a brick wall for my 3rd-great-grandmother who disappears after 1880."*

With the right prompt, AI becomes your **strategist**, not just your search engine.

It can suggest overlooked records based on era and location — like Freedmen's Bureau, land deeds, or voter rolls.

It can detect timeline gaps that hint at remarriage, migration, or reclassification.

Because when you pair ancestral instinct with logical pattern, the search gets sharper.

GENERATE A WORKING TASK LIST FOR ONGOING RESEARCH

One of the biggest challenges in genealogy isn't starting — it's picking back up after you've stepped away. Life happens, and without a clear task list, it's easy to forget where you left off. That's why creating a running checklist with AI can keep you grounded. It gives you a sense of direction every time you return to your research, so you're not starting over — you're building forward.

Ask:

"Based on the gaps in my tree, generate a checklist of next steps to explore."

Or:

"Turn these research questions into a to-do list with record types, locations, and dates to search."

You'll walk away with a **focused plan** you can return to every time you pick up your research again — no more wandering in circles.

That kind of structure turns casual searching into intentional legacy work.

You're not just hunting for names — you're mapping inheritance and identity.

When AI remembers where you left off, it helps preserve the rhythm of your momentum. And that rhythm matters when you're building something meant to last.

BONUS PROMPT IDEAS

Sometimes it's not about how much you ask — but how deeply you ask.

These prompts aren't just to help you get better at using AI. They're here to help you listen more closely to what your research is trying to reveal. When you're stuck or unsure, these kinds of questions can open new doors, uncover overlooked patterns, or confirm something your spirit already knew.

Try these when you need a shift in perspective, a spark of clarity, or a reminder that you're not doing this alone:

> "Create a timeline of every known event in this ancestor's life using the documents I've uploaded."

> "Which record sets have I overlooked for some-one

born in 1860 in Mississippi?"

"Help me write a research log entry for this session, including what I searched and what I found."

"Compare this ancestor's timeline with historical events that may have shaped their movements or identity."

"What patterns do you notice across multiple generations in this family line?"

"Which surnames appear consistently in this community over a 50-year span?"

"Based on this family's migration path, what county or parish should I search next?"

"Which individuals appear in both the 1880 and 1900 census in this household — and who's missing in between?"

These aren't just clever questions — they're keys.

Each one helps you unlock a layer you might have missed. When used with intention, prompts like these turn passive searching into guided discovery.

They invite AI to think with you, not just for you.

They help organize chaos into clarity, and fragments into a foundation.

Because this journey isn't just about finding people — it's about following the thread that reveals who they were, and how that truth lives in you.

STAY ROOTED IN PURPOSE

The ancestors aren't hiding — they're waiting on a plan.

They've left clues in courthouses, census rolls, oral stories, and soil. But gathering those pieces takes more than luck — it takes intention.

With AI, you no longer have to walk this path blindly.

This work is sacred. This calling is real.

You have a partner that helps you track where you've been, see what you missed, and guide you where to go next. You're not just building a tree — you're building a strategy.

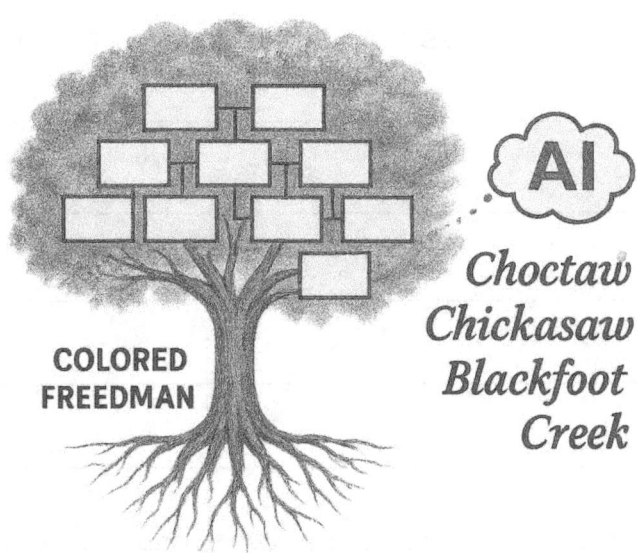

And like any good plan, it should stretch, evolve, and deepen as you grow. What confused you last year might feel clear today. What looked like a dead end might now be a doorway.

AI won't replace your intuition — it'll help you *trust* it.

It sharpens your focus, strengthens your rhythm, and reminds you that this journey was never random.

Let your research stay rooted in clarity, and your steps stay rooted in purpose.

Jot down any notes from this chapter to review later:

_____

_____

_____

_____

_____

_____

✳ Figure 22: **WORKSHEET: BUILDING A CUSTOM RESEARCH PLAN WITH AI — STEP-BY-STEP FLOW**

Use this worksheet to guide your AI assistant in creating a clear and culturally aligned genealogy research plan. Don't rush — this is about intention, not speed. Fill in what you know, and let the gaps show you where to dig deeper.

---

1. What Do You Want to Know?

Be specific. This is your "core question."

_____

_____

2. What Do You Already Know?

Include names, dates, places, or events that could anchor your search.

_____

_____

_____

3. What's Missing or Unclear?

List gaps, contradictions, or unknowns you want to resolve.

_____

_____

4. What Sources Could Help?

Name at least 3 potential records or collections. Think broad (e.g., Freedmen's Bureau, land deeds, tribal rolls, etc.).

1. _____
2. _____
3. _____

5. What's Your First Prompt to AI?

Draft a research-focused question or instruction you'd give to an AI tool.

"Using the details I've provided, help me find..."

_____
_____
_____

6. Next Steps (Based on AI Suggestions):

Summarize your next 1–3 research actions after reviewing AI's output.

1. _____
2. _____
3. _____

CHAPTER 13
Thirteen

Building a Family Timeline — The Blueprint for Clarity

One of the best ways to organize the chaos of Black genealogy is with a timeline. Timelines do what messy census pages and mismatched surnames can't — they help you see patterns, spot gaps, and rebuild a clearer story from scattered documents. When you combine timelines with AI, you can go even deeper.

Timelines are more than just dates. They give you structure, context, and sequence. And for Black American families — whose stories were often intentionally disjointed — this is everything.

When I began organizing my research, I found myself frustrated by contradictions: Someone was born in Mississippi but showed up in the Georgia census. A woman's age changed by 15 years across three documents. But when I started laying each record out year by year, it started coming together. Migration. Marriage. Reclassification. The timeline told the truth that the documents tried to hide.

This chapter will show you how to build timelines that reveal the truth — even when the records don't say it outright.

WHAT TO INCLUDE IN A GENEALOGY TIMELINE

A strong timeline doesn't need every record at once — it starts with a single known fact and expands outward. As you collect documents, stories, and locations, the structure begins to form. These aren't just dates and data points — they're proof of movement, survival, and identity. Every entry has a purpose, and when placed in sequence, they begin to speak.

Start with what you know — then build from there.

Here's what you can include:

- Birth and death dates (even approximate)

- Census entries (location, race classification, household members)
- Marriages, divorces, or changes in surname
- Land purchases or moves to new counties
- Church or school enrollments
- Employment or military service
- Key historical events that impacted your region (*e.g., Civil War, Reconstruction, Jim Crow laws*)

You're not just recording facts — you're telling the story of movement, survival, and identity.

HOW AI CAN HELP BUILD OR EXPAND A TIMELINE

Once your timeline is in motion, AI can help you speed up the process and spot things you might have missed. It may not hold the full story — but it can organize your details, flag contradictions, and offer suggestions based on patterns and regional history.

Think of it as your assistant, pulling pieces together so you can focus on the meaning behind the movement.

AI tools can be used to:

- Compare conflicting dates or records
- Calculate approximate birth years

- Fill in gaps based on regional migration trends
- Generate suggested events or locations based on nearby family members
- Highlight anomalies you might miss

Example Prompt:

"Using these records — 1880 census (Alabama), 1900 census (Georgia), 1917 draft card (Texas) — help me build a timeline for James M. Carter and highlight possible gaps or inconsistencies."

AI can pull the bones of a timeline together quickly. Then you come in and layer it with insight, context, and lived memory.

TIPS FOR USING TIMELINES STRATEGICALLY

Once your timeline starts taking shape, it's time to think like an investigator. Every date you enter should lead you somewhere. These aren't just events — they're signals. How you organize, annotate, and revisit your timeline can make the difference between hitting a wall and breaking through it. The more strategic you are, the more your timeline will speak back to you.

1. **Color-code for clarity** — Use different colors for different family members or types of events.
2. **Keep a notes column** — Jot down thoughts, questions, or theories next to each entry.

3. **Update as you go** — A timeline isn't static. It grows as your research grows.

4. **Let the gaps guide you** — Blank years aren't just missing data. They're research opportunities.

5. **Revisit with fresh eyes** — What didn't make sense last year might unlock something new today. Keep returning.

AI + TIMELINE = PATTERN RECOGNITION

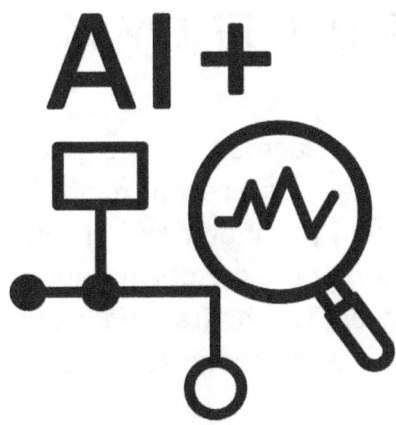

The real power of a timeline isn't just in what you put in — it's in what it reveals once everything is laid out. When you combine that with AI, you're not just organizing information… you're activating it.

AI can help you step back and see the bigger picture:

unexpected patterns, outliers, and connections you may have overlooked. This is where research becomes revelation.

Once you input enough data into a timeline, you can ask AI:

> "What patterns or inconsistencies do you see in this family's record over time?"

or

> "Can you suggest three possible reasons for the 10-year age gap between these two census entries?"

You'll be amazed what shows up.

REAL EXAMPLE FROM MY JOURNEY

Names can shape-shift across time, especially in the lines of Black American women. One record might call her a daughter, another a servant, and yet another might change her last name altogether. But when you slow down and map out the details — birth years, children, neighbors, and locations — you start to see through the fog and recognize the same woman hidden behind three names.

I had a woman in my line whose name changed three times across four decades. At first, I thought I had three different people. But when I laid out the timeline — birth year, children's names, consistent location — I realized it was one woman, not three. She'd been reclassified, remarried, and re-recorded.

She showed up as "Colored" in one census, "Mulatto" in another, and was eventually listed as "Negro" — but the children were the thread.

One child's name never changed across records, and that anchored everything.

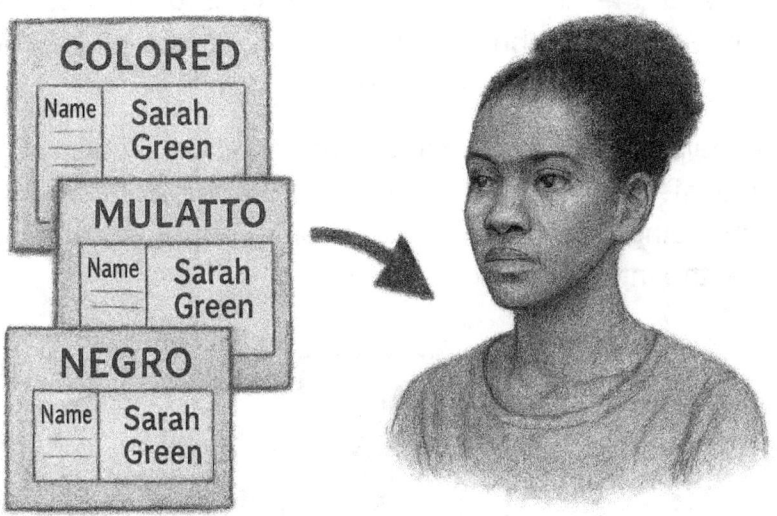

I cross-checked neighbors, midwife names, and even baptism records to confirm it.

The AI didn't catch the shift — I did, but it helped me organize the evidence.

It stacked the facts so I could see the story.

And that's how you turn data into identity.

That timeline not only cleared the confusion — it proved the lineage.

Next, let's discuss how timelines are living, visual scripts.

TIMELINES ARE YOUR STORYBOARDS

Think of your genealogy like a documentary. Each record is a scene, and the timeline is your storyboard — not just a sequence of facts, but a living, visual script of how your people moved, survived, and evolved.

AI can help you build it. It can line up the scenes and point out the inconsistencies. But it's your spirit, your insight, your lived understanding that gives the *story* voice. You are the narrator. You are the interpreter of memory.

And as you begin to see the full picture — not just names and dates, but journeys, choices, and turning points — something begins to shift. You're not just gathering history anymore.

You're restoring it.

You're reclaiming what was scattered, mis recorded, or erased.

You're bringing your people back into view — fully seen, fully known.

And when the story starts to take shape, so does the healing.

Let that healing guide your next steps.

The gaps will speak just as loudly as the facts — don't ignore them.

Sometimes what's missing is the loudest part of the story, pointing to a shift, a struggle, or a silence that was never meant to be permanent.

Every migration, name change, reclassification, or disappearance holds a rhythm — and when you slow down and trace it, that rhythm begins to reveal a hidden truth.

Now it's your turn to lay it all out.

Use the worksheet in **[Figure 23]** to start building your family's timeline — year by year, place by place, person by

Begin with what you know, then fill in the rest as more records come to light.

Don't worry about perfection. This is a living map. A blueprint for clarity.

This is more than research.

It's remembrance with intention.

Jot down any notes from this chapter to review later:

___

___

___

___

___

___

🌳 Figure 23: TIMELINE BUILDING WORKSHEET

Year	Name	Notes
	Event (eg. birth, death, marriage, migration)	

Figure 23: Timeline Building Worksheet - Track life events across time to spot patterns, gaps, and clues that can guide your next steps.

Timelines turn scattered facts into stories. Use this chart to organize what's known — and discover what's missing.

FEATURED AI TIP

Names don't always travel alone. Sometimes an occupation, location, or unique household detail can help confirm a match. AI can help you cross-reference unusual jobs, neighbor names, or birthplaces to verify identity.

AI Prompt: "Can you search for records with similar occupations, birthplaces, or neighbors to confirm if this is the same person?"

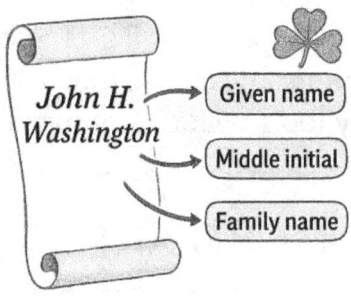

CHAPTER 14

Fourteen

Naming Patterns and Generational Codes — Recognizing Lineage Clues in the Names

One of the most powerful moments in genealogy is when scattered pieces begin to form a lineage — not just names on paper, but generations flowing into each other like branches of the same tree. But if you're researching Black American ancestry, those connections are rarely handed to you clean. They're hidden in vague census labels, buried in burial records, or whispered between surnames that were spelled differently in every decade.

This is the chapter where AI becomes more than a tool — it becomes your thinking partner. You've already gathered and organized your documents. Now it's time to dig deeper and **connect those generations**, especially the ones that traditional genealogy tools overlook or misclassify.

WHY THESE LINKS ARE HARDER FOR US TO SEE

Let's be real — Black American family research is uniquely complex. It's not just about missing records. It's about **how** we were recorded, **who** was doing the recording, and **why** certain truths were deliberately left out or disguised.

Our relatives were often:

- Listed as "servants," "boarders," or "farmhands" in households where they were actually family

- Moved across states between census years with no clear explanation

- Recorded with different surnames depending on the informant, the era, or the census taker's bias

- Split across multiple households due to migration, death, or forced displacement

But it goes deeper than that.

Sometimes, entire family lines were hidden in plain sight — absorbed into stepfamilies, renamed after remarriage, or simply marked "N.N." (no name) because someone didn't bother to ask. In other cases, names were changed for protection, survival, or reinvention. Spelling didn't matter. Accuracy wasn't the goal. And yet, within those inconsistent records, the truth still lingers.

So yes — these links are harder for us to see.

But just because the connections aren't obvious doesn't mean they aren't there.

You just have to know where — and how — to look.

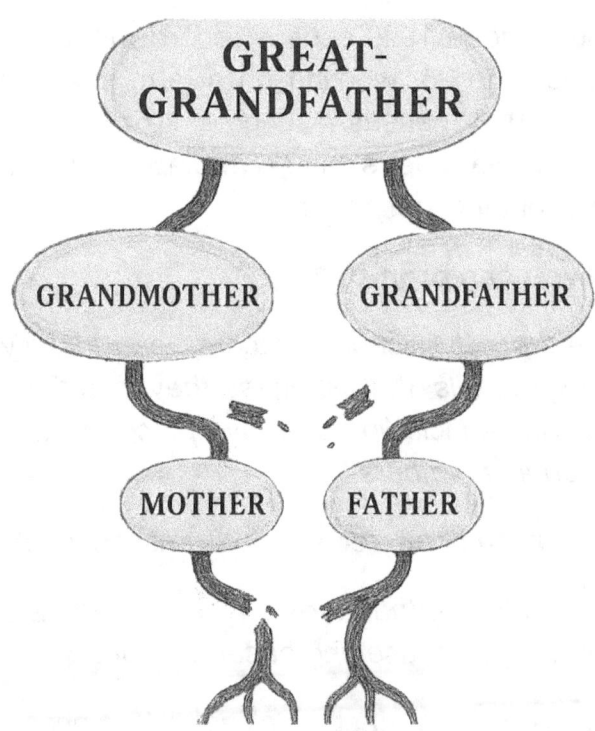

USING AI TO FIND WHO REAPPEARS IN YOUR RECORDS

Sometimes the same person shows up across different records — but with a slightly different name, age, or even race. You may not recognize them at first glance, but AI can help make those subtle connections visible. When you train it to look for patterns instead of perfect matches, you start to uncover how your relatives reappeared over time — renamed, relocated, or rewritten.

Let's say you've got a 1920 census record with a man named **Robert James**, age 25, working on a farm in Alabama. You also have a 1940 census listing a **Robert J. Reed** in Mississippi — similar age, similar birthplace. The names don't match exactly, but the story might.

Here's how you can prompt AI:

> *"Compare these two census records and identify any overlapping details that suggest they could be the same person — including age, birthplace, occupation, and household members."*

You can even upload both records (or transcriptions) and ask:

> *"Is there evidence that these two Roberts are the same man? Show reasoning based on context."*

AI will help you look past spelling differences or name changes to see patterns — like both men having a sister named Lula, or both being born in the same rural township.

REFLECTION: WHAT I LEARNED FROM THE NAMES IN MY LINEAGE

I'll be honest — I didn't always catch the name patterns at first. I was too busy looking for perfect matches. But then I started paying attention to initials, to middle names that only showed up in obituaries, and to nicknames passed down like heirlooms. That's when things shifted.

I realized that my great-grandfather wasn't missing. He had just been renamed. Rewritten. Folded into someone else's household with a different last name. But the first name... that stayed. His initials echoed through three generations — even when the surname changed.

That's how I knew I was getting close. That's how I knew he wanted to be found.

Names aren't just labels. In Black genealogy, they are codes — passed down, altered, hidden, but never fully erased. AI can help you spot those codes. But only you can recognize what they mean to your family's legacy.

These are the kinds of clues you don't always catch the first time. But with AI and intuition working together, patterns start to rise to the surface — even from the margins.

Once you start seeing the names — not just reading them —

you'll notice the echoes.

A middle initial that skips a generation. A name that reappears in a niece, a grandson, or a great-uncle whose story was barely told. These are the quiet threads that tie our lineages together.

You don't always realize it in the moment, but names leave trails. Sometimes they're loud — passed down with pride. Other times, they whisper — showing up quietly across decades. What looks like coincidence is often a sign that the story is still unfolding.

And it's not always the first names you need to look at — it's how they pair with surnames across time. A middle name might be someone's maiden name. An initial might match an uncle who died young. Even the order of names can signal family hierarchy or intention.

When a name appears "out of nowhere," it's often a message from somewhere. Ask yourself: who was this person named after? Who else carried that name? Who might have been forgotten — unless this name was their way of being remembered?

You'll begin to recognize naming as resistance, remembrance, and reclaiming — all hidden in plain sight. What seemed like just a list of names becomes a map of honor. A living thread.

That's the beauty of this work. We don't just find people. We recognize them.

Now, let's trace the echoes.

*Use the chart sample **[see Figure 24]** to trace how first names, middle names, and initials were passed down or transformed across generations.*

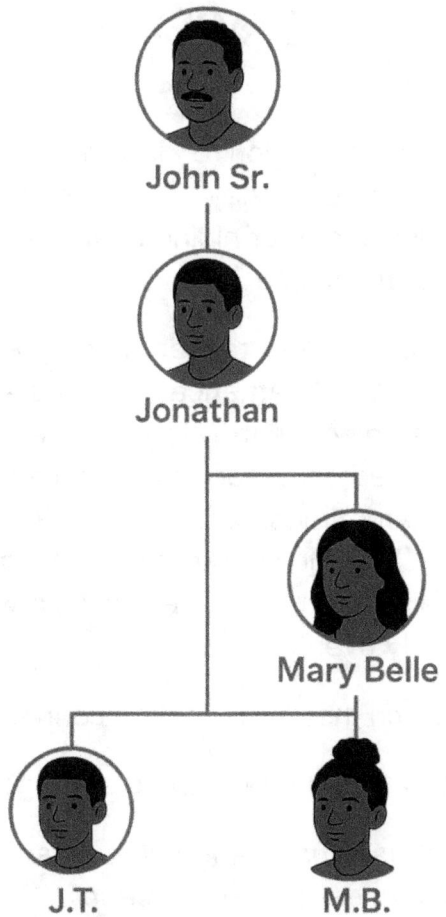

[Figure 24]: Names carry memory. Use this chart sample to trace how first names, middle names, and initials were passed down or transformed across generations — revealing patterns of honor, identity, and lineage.

FINDING FAMILY IN THE MARGINS: BOARDERS, NEIGHBORS, AND IN-LAWS

Sometimes, the person you're looking for isn't in the household you expected. They might be next door, listed under someone else's roof, or hiding behind a title that doesn't scream "family" at first glance.

One of the biggest mistakes researchers make — especially when working with Black American records — is assuming that everyone is listed where they "should" be. But our families were fluid. They lived together out of necessity, took each other in during hard times, and were often mislabeled in official documents. What looks like a servant could be a sister. What's listed as a boarder might be a cousin who just arrived from the next county over.

AI can help you catch those overlooked connections.

One of the best AI tricks I've used is asking:

"Look at this census page and tell me if any surnames or occupations repeat across households."

Or:

"Does anyone listed nearby share a surname, birthplace, or age range that suggests a family tie?"

✨ What AI Helped Me Uncover:

In one 1930 census, I found a woman listed as a "maid" in the household next door to a cousin. Her name didn't ring a bell at first, but when I asked AI to cross-check her against names in my existing tree, it flagged her as a previously undocumented sibling — misclassified as a domestic worker instead of family. Same age range. Same birthplace. Same surname in other records. She had been there the whole time — just hiding in plain sight.

Here's another thing to watch for:

Sometimes a familiar name shows up as a boarder or lodger across multiple census years — always near your family, never quite "in" the household. That's often a red flag. Ask yourself:

- ✓ Did they move together between counties?
- ✓ Do their children have overlapping names or ages?
- ✓ Were they witnesses on marriage licenses or co-owners of land?

Even burial plots can tell the truth. People who were "just neighbors" in the census often ended up buried side by side.

- ✓ Did they enlist together in war records or sign similar labor contracts?
- ✓ Is their race or classification listed differently depending on who recorded it?
- ✓ Were they listed as informants on each other's death certificates?

So when a name shows up more than once — even on the edges of the page — don't dismiss it. That might be the piece that fills the gap.

AI can help highlight those patterns. But only you can feel when something is too close to be coincidence.

SPOTTING SURNAME SHIFTS ACROSS TIME

A surname isn't always a straight line — sometimes it curves, splits, or gets rewritten altogether. For Black American families, a last name might reflect survival more than lineage. What shows up on one record may look unfamiliar on the next — but it's still yours.

AI can also help you catch surname shifts that occur across decades.

You might say:

> "Track every instance of this individual or household in the 1900, 1910, and 1920 census records, and flag any surname or spelling changes."

Why this matters? Because many Black families used multiple surnames — some tribal, some from former enslavers, some inherited from step-parents or guardians. AI can help track how these names evolve across generations. A surname might change due to who gave the information, reflect resistance or heritage, skip a generation, or resurface later — but every shift is a potential clue, not a mistake.

USING AI TO LINK OCCUPATION AND LOCATION PATTERNS

A less obvious but powerful connection comes from what your ancestors did and where they did it.

Let's say three men across 30 years were listed as blacksmiths in the same rural township. They have different names — but AI may flag them as connected due to shared location, occupation, and age range.

What might seem like coincidence to the eye can become a clear pattern when AI reviews the data as a whole. These aren't just job titles — they're breadcrumbs of legacy, often passed down through apprenticeship or family skillsets. If you see repeated occupations in the same area, there's a good chance you're looking at a family trade — not random duplication.

Try prompting AI to:

"Look at these three records. Could the occupation and address suggest these men were related?"

Or ask:

"Does the fact that they lived within the same 5-mile radius over 40 years support a generational link?"

This is especially helpful for tracking families who worked land over generations — farmers, washerwomen, carpenters — roles often passed down even when names did not.

PROMPT TEMPLATES FOR THIS CHAPTER

Here are a few ready-made AI prompts to help you dig for generational clues:

> "Compare these two people across different census years. What suggests they might be the same?"

> "Find shared surnames or relationships across these three households."

> "Can you cross-reference this burial record with census data to find next of kin?"

> "Group all individuals with this surname by decade and location."

> "List all children born to women with this surname between 1880–1920 in Mississippi."

> "Show every instance where this surname appears with a middle name or initial — highlight patterns."

You can also use prompts to test assumptions and reveal what the records aren't showing. Ask AI to highlight gaps in a timeline or to flag households that seem incomplete.

Use it to surface unusual naming patterns that might signal reclassification or blended families.

Don't be afraid to run the same record through multiple prompt angles. That's where deeper connections often appear.

AI CAN'T SEE SPIRIT — BUT YOU CAN

Even as AI helps you make these connections, never forget: **you are the decoder**, not the machine. AI can't feel when a name "rings true." It can't recognize a nickname your grandmother used to say. It can't sense when a certain surname shows up too often to be coincidence. But you can.

So, use AI for what it does best — pattern recognition, data comparison, record alignment — and let your spirit guide the rest.

This chapter is about seeing what's been fragmented — and pulling it back together with clarity, patience, and ancestral intuition. Our families weren't broken — they were *scattered.*

These hidden links and household clues are the breadcrumbs they left for us to follow.

And now you have the tools to see what they always hoped someone would find.

Now it's your turn to map the codes. Use this worksheet **[Figure 25]** to track which names show up again and again — even when the spelling, surname, or form changes. List first names, nicknames, middle initials, and any details you've noticed across generations. This isn't just about memory. It's about recognition.

You're not just looking for matches — you're tracing legacy.

Figure 25: NAMING PATTERNS AND GENERATIONAL CODES

FIRST/MIDDLE/LAST NAMES	KNOWN NICKNAMES OR INITIALS	APPROX YEAR OF BIRTH	NOTES

Figure 25: Naming Patterns and Generational Codes Worksheet. Name patterns are not a coincidence — they're a code. Track them, record them, and let the lineage reveal itself.

FEATURED AI TIP

The record might list them as a servant, laborer, or inmate — but that's not all they were. AI can help you look beyond the label by connecting records that reveal their full story.

AI Prompt: "*Can you find other records connected to this person that show their life outside of this label or institution?*"

CHAPTER 15

We Been Had Names — Uncovering Generational Naming Codes and Surname Truths with AI

Before the world gave us numbers, before they reclassified us and renamed us, we had names — strong names, meaningful names, names that echoed across generations even when the paper trail didn't.

Yes, many of the enslaved took on the surnames of the so-called masters. But what's rarely said is that many of those enslavers weren't even using their own birth names. They, too, were adopting surnames — some taken from tribal communities, Indigenous nations, or colonial lineages already established here in the Americas. In other words, the names themselves were recycled, renamed, and repurposed long before they landed in our records.

So when you're tracing Black American lineage, you're not just dealing with scattered or misspelled names. You're dealing with layers —some taken, some forced, some hidden, and others reclaimed. Some were chosen to honor land or legacy.

Some were stripped down to fit into a system that didn't want us to remember.

This chapter isn't just about what we were called — it's about what we called ourselves. And with AI, we now have the tools to decode those naming patterns, recover hidden surnames, and reconnect with naming traditions that predate colonization.

THE MYTH OF THE "GIVEN SURNAME"

There's a common genealogy myth that says:

"Black people got their last names from their enslavers after emancipation."

That's only partially true — and dangerously oversimplified. Many of our surnames:

- Came from **tribal names or spiritual titles** long before slavery
- Were chosen deliberately **after freedom** to honor family, land, or dignity
- Were **passed down from free Black communities** who maintained their identity despite the system

But over time, records were altered, spellings changed, and names were **flattened into Eurocentric molds**.

Some names were Anglicized versions of Indigenous terms, while others were government-imposed labels meant to erase lineage.

Even when a name seems 'common,' it may carry regional or spiritual meaning that AI won't catch without cultural context.

That's why the AI tools we use must go deeper than just transcription. We're not just tracing names — we're **reviving memory**.

HOW AI CAN HELP DECODE NAMING PATTERNS

Our ancestors didn't always have the luxury of paperwork — but they left clues in what they named, renamed, and passed down. Names became maps, messages, and memorials. But over time, those names were scrambled by systems that didn't care about legacy. AI can't restore the memory for you — but it can help you organize what's already echoing in your line. When used right, it becomes a lens to uncover naming cycles, tribal roots, and patterns that were hidden beneath generations of misclassification.

Here's how to use AI to start making sense of the naming chaos:

🔄 1. Ask AI to Group Names Across Generations

If you upload a list of people in your family tree (first name, last name, year of birth), **try this:**

"Group these names by surname, and highlight those that repeat every other generation. Do any middle names show up as surnames later?"

This helps you spot **naming cycles** — like when a grandfather's first name becomes a grandson's middle name.

In Black American families, this was often done to honor elders when there were no legal wills or land deeds.

2. Ask AI To Compare Tribal And Family Surnames

You can ask:

"Do any of these surnames appear in tribal registries, Dawes Rolls, or Southeastern Native groups?"

Or:

"Which of these surnames were common among the Choctaw, Creek, or Cherokee Freedmen?"

You might be surprised to find that a name passed down in your family matches a name on an Indigenous roll — not because you were "given" that name, but because it was **yours** to begin with.

Ask AI which tribal surnames were reclassified or misspelled over time.

Check for name variants across different census years — especially in areas with high Native presence.

And if a surname disappears for a generation, look for it on a different racial classification line.

 **Real-Life Example:**

> # This wasn't a name we were given. It was a name we kept.
>
> – On tracing the Reed surname back to Choctaw and Chickasaw lands.

In my own tree, I asked AI to cross-check the surname **REED** with known tribal registries in Mississippi. What came back wasn't just a match — it was a revelation. Several Reed families were listed in connection with **Choctaw and Chickasaw lands**, all within the same counties and timeframes my people had lived. On paper, they were classified as "Black" or "Negro." But in the tribal records, those same surnames showed up under a different lens — families connected to land, lineage, and nations that existed before statehood.

That one query led me to a deeper truth I had already felt in my bones:

This wasn't a name we were given. It was a name we kept.

What AI confirmed was what memory had already whispered — that our names weren't random or borrowed, they were **remnants of something older**, something sacred. That moment didn't just shift my research — it shifted my relationship to the Reed name. It no longer represented a break in the line.

It became a bridge.

🔍 3. Investigate Nicknames and "Middle Name Swaps"

AI can help you uncover when:

- A person named **"Lula May Smith"** becomes **"May L. Smith"** in another record
- A grandfather called **"Bud"** was actually named **"James Sr."**
- **Initials like R.J. or T.M.** are dropped entirely from certain records
- Someone listed as "Junior" later appears with a completely different first name
- A middle name becomes the child's first name in the next generation
- An obituary uses a nickname the census never recorded — revealing the missing link

Prompt example:

> "Compare these three names — Lula M. Smith, May Lula Smith, and Lula Mae Smythe — and determine if they could refer to the same individual based on year, location, and known relatives."

CULTURAL CODES IN OUR NAMES

Names were never just names in our communities — they were declarations. Sometimes they spoke of spirit. Sometimes they whispered royalty, survival, or land. Even when our families weren't allowed to pass down wealth or property, they passed down *meaning* through what they named us. The deeper you look, the more you'll find that Black American names weren't random — they were coded. And those codes tell us who we were, who we are, and who we refused to forget.

Black American names often carried cultural clues:

- ✓ **Biblical names** for spiritual grounding (Isaiah, Elijah, Mary, Ruth)

- ✓ **Royal names** to reclaim stolen dignity (King, Prince, Queenie, Noble)

- ✓ **Initials-only names** used when the full name was undocumented or intentionally hidden

- ✓ **Tribal-sounding names** that survived through phonetic memory, even when their origins were forgotten (Ayanna, Omari, Talib, Zahra)

- ✓ **Names inspired by elders or ancestors** that reappear across generations (Mama Annie Mae, Papa Joe, Aunt Frances)

- ✓ **Location-based names** that tied families to a place or migration story (Georgia, Tex, Carolina, Delta)

- ✓ **Virtue-based names** that reflected hopes and values (Charity, Patience, Faith, Hope)

- ✓ **Unique spellings or invented names** that served as resistance — a declaration of identity that couldn't be easily erased

AI can help you **group and translate these names** in a way that exposes the soul of the naming tradition.

Try this prompt:

"Categorize these first names by theme: biblical, tribal, nature, or royal."

It's more than organization — it's recovery of meaning.

Below **[Figure 26]** is a generational name chart based on real patterns found in Black American families. As you review, notice how names evolve across generations — sometimes repeating, sometimes shifting — and how these cycles reveal hidden codes of remembrance.

Uncovering Generational Naming Codes and Surname Truths with AI

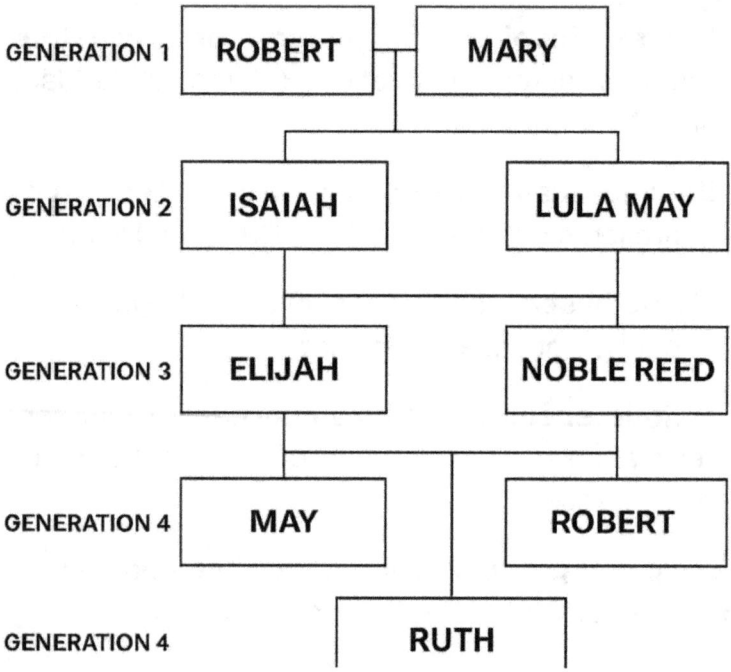

Figure 26: Generational Naming Pattern — Surnames, Middle Names, and First Name Repetition Across Time

Names don't just repeat — they carry rhythm, honor, and intention. This chart shows how naming patterns evolved across generations, revealing hidden codes, cultural memory, and the quiet ways our families preserved identity even when the records didn't.

RECLAIMING THE TRUTH ABOUT "SLAVE NAMES"

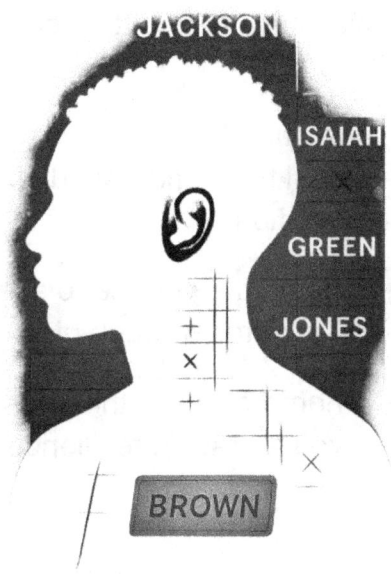

The term "slave name" has been repeated so often that many have accepted it without question. But names carry deeper histories than the systems that tried to erase them. Not every surname came from bondage — and even those that did were reshaped, redefined, and re-rooted by the very people who bore them.

What's been lost in mainstream narratives is the truth that many Black Americans preserved power through names — power that wasn't given, but rebuilt. With the help of AI, we can retrace those threads and reclaim what was never truly lost.

We hear this phrase a lot:

"I want to get rid of my slave name."

But what if the name wasn't always from slavery? What if it was a **reclaimed tribal title**, or a name **kept alive** through generations of resistance? What if the name has power — not because of who gave it to you, but because of how your ancestors carried it?

Sometimes a surname that looks simple on paper carries layers of meaning — tribal ties, land-based identity, or survival through forced reclassification.

AI can help you dig beneath the surface to see how that name traveled, changed, and endured through historical shifts.

When you analyze a name through this lens, you're not just chasing etymology — you're tracing resilience.

Using AI, you can:

- **Trace the name's transformation** over decades
- **Identify geographic hotspots** where the name was common
- **Reveal the family connections** that made the name sacred
- **Compare how the name appears** in different record types (census, probate, marriage, etc.)
- **Detect spelling variations** that reflect migration, education, or clerical error
- **Map the name's presence** across generations in one region

PROMPT TEMPLATES TO USE RIGHT NOW

"Group these names by spelling variation and note any overlaps by decade."

"Map the migration pattern of this surname from 1850 to 1950."

"List surnames from this family that appear in both Black and Native American registries."

"What is the most likely origin of the surname 'Noble' in Alabama in the 1880s?"

25	REED
38	WASHINGTON
30	BROWN
19	FREEMON —
42	CARTER Laborer
30	~~NOBLE~~
40	GREEN
48	JACKSON

We never lost our names — they were buried, fragmented, and mislabeled. But they never stopped echoing through our bloodlines. Every Robert, Lula, Noble, Isaiah, Queenie, and May was part of a deeper pattern — a rhythm — that our people carried with or without permission.

Now you have the tools to **uncover those patterns, speak those names aloud, and honor the code** your family left behind.

And remember: *We didn't just "get" names — we gave them meaning.*

Now it's your turn to dig into the names in your own lineage. Use the worksheet **[Figure 27]** to document repeating names, spelling variations, middle initials, and any cultural or tribal ties you suspect.

Watch for echoes, hidden codes, and generational rhythms that reveal how your family preserved identity through every reclassification and mislabeling.

List repeating names, spelling variants, middle initials, and possible cultural or tribal ties.

This is more than a worksheet. It's a key.

And these aren't just names — they're signals.

Figure 27: NAME DOCUMENTING WORKSHEET

FIRST NAMES	MIDDLE NAMES & INITIALS	NICKNAMES	NAME MEANINGS

Figure 27: Name Documenting Worksheet. Use this chart to track patterns, honor legacy, and reclaim the meaning that was always there.

SURNAMES THAT ECHOED THROUGH THE FREEDMEN ERA — A FOUNDATION FOR AI ANALYSIS

Before DNA swabs and shaky leaf hints, our ancestors' names were written in ledgers, contracts, deposit slips, and court petitions. These names weren't just labels — they were remnants of identity, memory, and survival. From the labor contracts of the Freedmen's Bureau to the deposit slips of the Freedmen's Bank, Black American surnames began to appear in official records — many for the first time — in the decades following emancipation.

But those names didn't come out of nowhere.

Some were kept from before the fall of slavery. Others were chosen to honor land, tribe, or family. And still others were imposed and then reclaimed. These names hold stories — and now, with AI, we can trace them with sharper focus and deeper clarity.

The following chart is a curated list of surnames pulled from real historical documents tied to Black Americans in the 19th and early 20th centuries — including Freedmen's Bureau records, Freedmen's Bank depositors, and the Dawes Rolls of tribal Freedmen.

This is not a complete list. But it is a powerful starting point — a foundation for AI-powered surname validation and ancestral alignment.

Use this chart to:

- Spot recurring surnames in your family tree
- Cross-check with tribal registries and land allotments
- Track regional surname clusters by decade
- Uncover misclassified ancestors hiding behind familiar names

📄 A–Z SURNAME INDEX (FREEDMEN ERA, SAMPLE)

A — Allen, Amos, Archer, Askew

B — Brown, Bynum, Boykin, Blue

C — Carter, Coleman, Crockett, Chatman

D — Davis, Durham, Dorsey, Drew

E — Edwards, Eaton, Epps, Elam

F — Foster, Franklin, Frazier, Fields

G — Green, Griffin, Glover, Gaines

H — Harris, Hodge, Hunter, Hightower

I — Ingram, Ivy, Isaacs, Irvin

J — Johnson, Jackson, Jones, Jeffries

K — King, Kelly, Kennedy, Kirk

L — Lewis, Lee, Long, Lawson

M — Moore, Mitchell, Murphy, McGee

N — Nelson, Noble, Norman, Newsom

O — Owens, Oliver, Overton, Outlaw

P — Parker, Price, Perkins, Pruitt

Q — Quinn, Quick, Quarles, Queen

R — Reed, Robinson, Ross, Randle

S — Smith, Scott, Stewart, Sorrell

T — Taylor, Thomas, Thornton, Tucker

U — Underwood, Upshaw, Utley, Upton

V — Vaughn, Valentine, Vinson, Vance

W — Williams, Washington, Walker, Wilkins

X — (Rare — may appear as initials like "X" adopted post-emancipation)

Y — Young, Yancy, Yarborough, York

Z — Zachary, Ziegler, Zeno, Zane

These names are more than entries — they are echoes.

Each one carries the memory of a people who survived reclassification, relocation, and record-wiping.

Some were names chosen in freedom, others imposed in bondage — but all became part of our legacy.

Use this list as a guide, but let your intuition and ancestral memory lead the search.

Because when a surname makes your spirit pause — that's not coincidence. That's calling.

🧠 AI PROMPTS FOR USING THE FREEDMEN SURNAME LIST

Use these sample prompts to connect the surnames above to deeper research. You're not just looking for a match — you're looking for movement, repetition, regional clues, and ancestral alignment.

📁 Prompt #1: Group and Compare

"Group these surnames by frequency in my family tree. Which ones appear more than once across generations?"

🎈 Prompt #2: Map the Movement

"Can you map the migration of the surname 'Reed' across Mississippi and Alabama from 1870 to 1930 using census and Freedmen records?"

📜 Prompt #3: Match with Tribal Records

"Do any of these surnames appear in the Cherokee or Choctaw Freedmen Dawes Rolls? List counties and family heads if available."

🧬 Prompt #4: Cross-Check for Lineage, Not Imitation

"Compare the surname 'Jackson' in Alabama Freedmen's Bank records versus its appearance in post-1970 immigration records in New York. Are these likely the same lineage?"

📖 Prompt #5: Track Generational Naming Patterns

"Which of these surnames also appear as middle names or first names in this family tree? Highlight recurring usage across decades."

Even a familiar name doesn't guarantee a familiar bloodline. What matters is the pattern — the repetition, the region, the rhythm. The surnames in this list are not just names — they are echoes from a time when our ancestors were reclaiming who they were, often on their own terms. AI can help you follow those echoes and separate what was inherited from what was imitated.

Before you continue, take a moment to write down a few prompts of your own for searching the Freedmen Surname List.

- **Prompt 1:**

_____

_____

- **Prompt 2:**

_____

_____

CHAPTER 16
Sixteen

They Speak Like Us But They Ain't Us — Using AI to Spot Language and Surname Cosplay in Genealogy

---

You ever hear somebody use our words, but something just feels off?

- They say "sis," but it don't carry the same weight.

- They say "woke," but not from the place we meant it.
- They wear the slang like a costume — not a memory.

That's the thing about Black American language: it's not just vocabulary — it's vibration. It's history wrapped in rhythm. It's grief coded into laughter. It's survival turned into melody. We've always spoken in a way that holds more than just meaning — it holds memory.

So when others try to imitate it, it falls flat. Because they weren't forged in it. They didn't grow up with a mother who called you "chile" one minute and "baby" the next. They didn't live the layered code-switching that lets you speak one way at school, another in the house, and a third when your spirit needs to be heard.

This chapter isn't about guarding identity — it's about tracing it. Because names and language might be copied, but lineage leaves a pattern. And now, we have AI tools to find it.

USING AI TO SPOT IMITATION IN SURNAMES AND SPEECH PATTERNS

In the age of digital genealogy, a surname alone isn't enough to confirm lineage. Just because a person has a name like *Jackson, Harris,* or *Reed* doesn't mean they're connected to your line — or even your culture. AI can help you detect when a name is being **used**, not **inherited**. Here's how.

🧬 **1. Ask AI to Group Surnames by Geographic and Cultural Context**

You can feed AI a list of surnames and ask:

> "Which of these surnames appear most frequently in Black American records prior to 1900?"

> "Which of these surnames were common among post-1960 immigrants in New York, Georgia, or California?"

This helps separate names with deep roots from those recently adopted. You'll often find that a name that *looks* familiar actually entered your area through a completely different path — a different family, a different migration, a different story.

2. Compare Census Locations, Not Just Names

When you're unsure whether a surname truly belongs to your lineage — or just passes through it — location is your best clue. The land holds memory, and families that are rooted tend to leave patterns behind. Even when names shift in spelling, the soil remembers who stayed. AI can help you trace those footprints across time.

Try asking AI:

> "Track this surname across the 1900, 1910, and 1920 censuses. Did it stay in the same county or move across states?"

True lineage leaves footprints. If a name has been present in your ancestral county for generations — even with spelling changes — that's a sign of rootedness. But if the name shows up suddenly post-immigration or jumps regions every decade, that may signal a different origin.

3. Use AI to Detect Cultural Mismatch in Language Use

Black American speech isn't just about what's said — it's how it's said, *why* it's said, and who it was meant for. Our language holds rhythm, breath, and cultural memory that outsiders can't quite capture, even when they try.

When reviewing written records or interviews, there are times when the words might look right on the surface... but something underneath feels off.

That's where AI can help you spot what doesn't align with the lived experience of your people.

While AI can't "hear" tone, it can read inconsistencies.

It can also flag when a record was likely written *about* your ancestors — not *by* them — which helps you weigh its accuracy.

Try:

> *"Compare the writing style and terminology used in these two interview transcripts. Do they reflect consistent Black American vernacular usage?"*

IT'S NOT ABOUT EXCLUSION. IT'S ABOUT **ACCURACY**

If we don't distinguish between cultural imitation and ancestral reality, we risk misclassifying relatives, inserting false lines, or allowing borrowed names to overwrite inherited ones. And when we blur the lines between what was lived and what was copied, we lose more than clarity — we lose legacy.

This isn't about gatekeeping identity. It's about protecting the rhythm, the memory, and the truth that's been carried through your bloodline for generations. Because the moment you start inserting imitation into your tree, you're no longer documenting your ancestors — you're documenting someone else's performance.

There's a difference between shared experience and shared lineage — and AI can't always tell the two apart.

Just because a record "looks right" doesn't mean it belongs to your line.

Cultural proximity isn't proof of connection. You still need documentation, patterns, and confirmation.

And when you stay rooted in discernment, you honor the ones who lived it — not the ones who copied it.

And that's what makes AI powerful when paired with discernment — it can show you the traces, but only you can recognize the truth.

🔍 PROMPT TEMPLATES FOR CULTURAL AND SURNAME VERIFICATION

Now that you understand how AI can highlight patterns that don't quite add up, it's time to put that into action. Below are a few focused prompts you can use when you're questioning

whether a surname, speech pattern, or cultural marker is genuinely tied to your lineage — or possibly adopted.

Try asking AI:

> "Group these surnames by geographic origin and note any that appear in both Black American and recent immigrant records."

> "Does this surname appear in any Freedmen's Bureau, Dawes Rolls, or Black church records before 1920?"

> "Compare naming patterns across these census entries."

> "Flag surnames that appear only after 1965 in this state and identify likely immigration origins."

> "Analyze the phrasing used in these two interviews.

Which one reflects more consistent Black American vernacular?"

These aren't just tech tricks — they're tools to protect your lineage from distortion. **AI can't feel the difference**, but it can help you prove what your spirit already knows: *every echo ain't ancestral.*

🪨 FOLLOW THE SHIFT, NOT JUST THE NAME

It's not always about who has the name — it's about how the name moved.

In Black genealogy, real lineage often shows up through slow, steady presence: generations living in the same parish, names passed between cousins, nicknames becoming middle names across time. But imitation moves differently. It jumps regions. It appears suddenly. It doesn't carry the echoes.

AI helps you follow those movements with precision.

Try this approach when you're unsure about a line in your research:

> *"Compare the migration trail of the surname 'Jefferson' across Georgia and Mississippi between 1870 and 1940. Does it follow consistent family structures, or does it appear in separate waves?"*

> *Or:*

> *"Map the surname 'Ali' in this region. When does it first*

appear in census records, and does it align with immigration data or Black American family continuity?"

These types of prompts let you analyze **movement patterns**, **naming frequency**, and **entry points** — all key signs of whether a name is tied to heritage or posturing.

 DOUBLE-CHECKING THE "CULTURAL MARKERS"

Ancestral name trail

Imitation name trail

Some records will list people as Black based on appearance — but that doesn't mean they're Black American. Cultural clues like:

- Funeral programs with no known relatives
- Surnames that don't show up until recent decades
- First names that mimic ours but don't repeat across

generations can reveal when someone was added into the category, not born from it.

When a name feels familiar but something doesn't quite line up, don't ignore that feeling — investigate it. That's where AI becomes a tool, not a trap. It won't tell you who's who on its own, but it will show you the patterns, overlaps, and silences that deserve a closer look.

AI can help you analyze documents across timeframes — but only if you ask the right questions. Try these prompts when a name looks familiar but the details feel off. You're not just searching — you're verifying.

> "Compare the obituary records of these individuals with similar surnames. Are there consistent family members, churches, or burial grounds mentioned?"

or

"How many times does this surname appear in Black church or school rosters before 1950?"

Use prompts like these to go beyond surface matches. Let AI help you check for continuity, location, repetition, and connection. Because sometimes the name is right — but the story is not. What looks like a match on paper might not match in memory — and AI helps bridge that gap.

In **[Figure 25],** Use the worksheet to document surnames, first names, and cultural patterns that show up in your research — especially when something feels off. Track how names move across time, how they change in spelling or context, and whether they align with your family's known migration path, vernacular style, or generational flow.

- Ask AI to compare surnames across generations, and flag entries where a name jumps location without logical movement.
  - Prompt it to identify when a family name appears with a sudden race reclassification or household role change — these are often signs of forced erasure.
  - Request a timeline of every appearance of a name across census records and see if it tracks with oral history.
  - Use AI to search for sound-alike variants when names were phonetically spelled by census takers unfamiliar with the culture.
  - Let it help you differentiate between bloodline and borrowed names — especially when two families in the

same town share a surname but nothing else.

- Train it to prioritize your family's context, not just what looks statistically "likely."
- And above all, remind it that memory holds more truth than math ever will.

Don't ignore your intuition just because the records seem to line up. If something doesn't sit right, it probably isn't. Your spirit knows what familiarity feels like — and AI is simply here to support, not override, that knowing.

This isn't just about identifying who isn't us — it's about protecting who is.

Jot down any notes from this chapter to review later:

_____

_____

_____

_____

❋ Figure 28: SURNAME AND LANGUAGE PATTERN ANALYSIS WORKSHEET

1. Surname / First Name Being Tracked:

2. First Appears In (Year / Record Type / Location):

3. Locations Where This Name Clustered:

4. Spelling Variations:

5. Associated Families or Households:

6. Common Prefixes, Suffixes, or Nicknames (e.g., "Mc," "De," "-son"):

7. Associated Language Patterns or Dialects (Creole, Gullah, etc.):

8. Were They Reclassified (Indian, Mulatto, Colored, Negro)?

☐ Yes   ☐ No   ☐ Not Sure

Notes: _____

9. Does the Name Appear on Tribal Rolls or Freedmen Records?

☐ Yes   ☐ No   ☐ Needs Research

Details: _____

10. Cultural / Vernacular Notes:

_____

11. AI Insights or Flags

_____

12. AI Prompt to Try:

> "Track all instances of the surname *[insert name]* from 1850–1930 in Mississippi, including spelling variations and appearance in Indian, Freedmen, or census rolls."

_____

Figure 28: Surname and Language Pattern Analysis Worksheet. Not every name that looks like ours comes from our line. Use this chart to track surnames and naming patterns across time, locations, and documents — and let AI help you separate mimicry from memory

FEATURED AI TIP

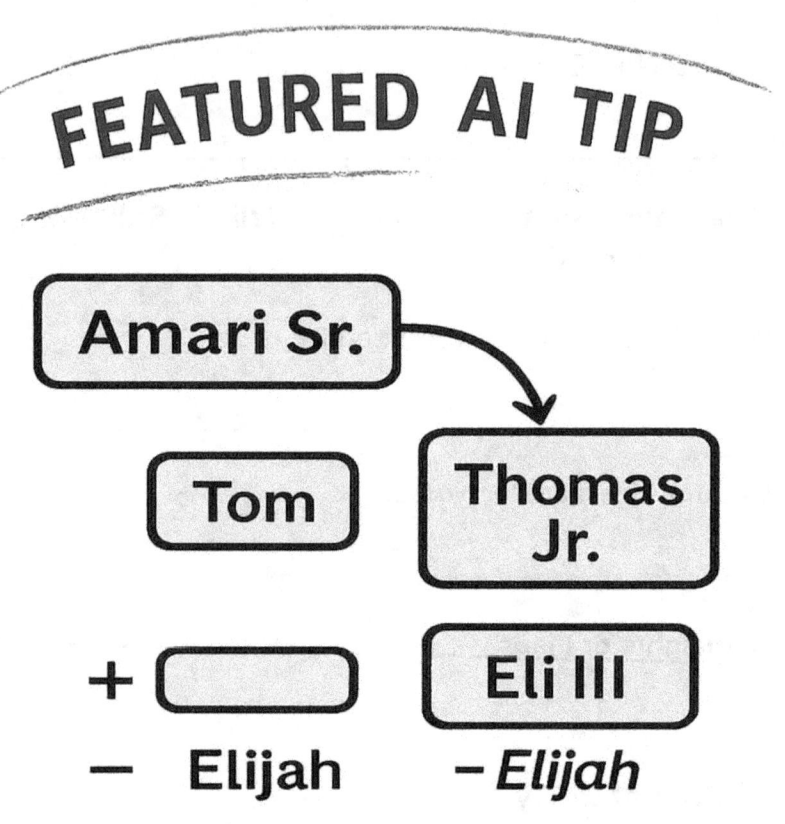

When a name repeats, shortens, or shifts slightly, it's not random — it's generational coding. Use AI to trace these naming patterns across time. What looks like a nickname might be the key to unlocking a whole branch.

CHAPTER 17

Seventeen

You Can't Fake This: The Culture Code of Black Americans

There's a rhythm to being Black American — and it can't be copied. You either know the beat, or you don't.

You either felt it in the kitchen growing up, in the way your auntie side-eyed somebody at church, or in the way your uncle used silence as a full sentence — or you didn't.

That's the difference between culture and cosplay.

Because while others can adopt the look, borrow the slang, and even take the names — what they can't replicate is the lived frequency of it. The unspoken. The instinct. The nuance.

This chapter isn't about comparison — it's about confirmation.

It's about recognizing the *invisible markers* of Black American lineage — the cultural codes passed through tradition, tone, taste, timing, and touch. Not the surface-level mimicry, but the deep, inherited knowing that you can't Google or graft.

And in a time when more people are trying to **blend in**, AI can help you protect what can't be faked.

WHAT CULTURE REVEALS THAT DNA CAN'T

DNA *can tell you what you're made of* — *but not what made you.*

It won't tell you the story behind why we always make a to-go plate at funerals.

It can't explain why your grandmother saved the good towels for company.

It won't recognize the sacredness of the hot comb, the HBCU shout, or that moment in church when the tambourine hits and you know the Spirit just shifted.

That's culture — not code.

This is why cultural codes matter in genealogy research.

Because if all you're looking at are genetic markers or surnames, you'll miss the deeper signal. You'll overlook that the name "Queenie" shows up three times in your maternal line.

Or that the men in your family have always been barbers, but never took a shop outside the block.

These aren't just coincidences. They're *continuities*.

AI can't experience these things, but it can help you track them:

- Which names repeat in your family even when the spelling changes?
- Which recipes are tied to women who show up on the same land across three censuses?
- Which phrases or terms of endearment show up in Freedmen narratives that your grandmother also used?

Try prompting AI:

"List all first names that appear in at least three generations in this family tree."

"Identify occupation clusters by generation and region. Are there repeating roles across time?"

"Compare these oral history quotes with documented phrases from WPA interviews. What language overlaps?"

It's not about proving culture with AI — it's about revealing the trace.

And once you spot the trace, you start to realize: they can speak like us.

But they still ain't us.

Because language can be mimicked, but lineage can't be faked.

They might borrow the slang, wear the style, or even adopt the surnames — but what they lack is the lived memory that shaped it.

There's a rhythm in our culture that wasn't learned — it was inherited.

AI can help surface the details, but only you can recognize when something doesn't carry the same weight.

That's why this work is sacred — because you're not just tracking names. You're protecting the code.

EXAMPLES OF COSPLAY — WHEN THE VIBE EXPOSES THE LIE

It's one thing to wear *our* style. It's another to carry *our* story.

We've reached a moment where outsiders are slipping into our culture like it's a costume — mimicking the slang,

posting the plates, and performing the experience. But the cracks always show.

- You see it when someone claims "soul food," but grabs kale instead of collards.

- You hear it when they try to revive slang they never lived through.

- You feel it when they speak on our struggles, but their roots don't trace back past a visa application.

That's the cosplay. It looks familiar — until it doesn't.

They can echo the sound, but not the soul.

They mimic the music, but they don't know the beat was born in bondage and brilliance. And AI? It can help you track the difference — when the cultural signal says one thing, but the records tell another.

REAL-WORLD PROMPT EXAMPLES

When you're not sure if a name, a voice, or a tradition is *ours*, you don't just look at the surface — you follow the pattern. You trace how it moved. You track when it appeared. You compare it to what your spirit already knows. And now, with AI, you can go deeper than guessing. You can test it against the records — and see what aligns with inheritance, and what feels like imitation.

These prompts are designed to help you do just that — to move past the performance and into the pattern. Use them to question what doesn't sit right, to verify what does, and to protect your lineage from distortion.

Because not everything that sounds familiar is kin. And not every cousin is cut from your root.

AI might notice a similarity — but only you will know if it truly resonates with your line.

The more familiar you become with your family's rhythms, the easier it is to spot what doesn't belong.

Let AI highlight the possible — then let your discernment confirm the truth.

> "Cross-reference this person's surname with immigration records and Black landownership rolls in Alabama between 1870–1920. Are there overlaps?"

> "Compare the migration path of these three surnames. Which stayed rooted in the South across generations, and which arrived post-1970?"

> "Which of these interview transcripts reflect Black American vernacular from WPA or Freedmen's narratives, and which deviate?"

> Analyze this list of surnames. Which are commonly linked to tribal rolls, which appear in freedmen records, and which show up primarily post-reclassification?

Culture speaks in patterns — and AI can help you decode when those patterns are authentic, and when they're manufactured. Because it's not just about calling out what's fake — it's about protecting what's real. It's about ensuring that our language, our surnames, our migrations, and our memories are not diluted or overwritten. With the right prompts, you're not just researching — you're guarding the vibration of your lineage.

And every time you follow that instinct to double-check, to trace it back, to feel the difference — you're doing the sacred work of keeping the frequency pure.

YOU CAN'T JUST COPY THE CULTURE — BECAUSE YOU DIDN'T LIVE THE CODES

There are things you can't fake — no matter how well you rehearse.

You can Google the recipes, wear the headwrap, recite the slogans... but if you didn't grow up with that plastic-covered couch, if you never got your hair greased while sitting between somebody's knees, if you never had to explain why the *real* new year starts in the spring — then you might speak the words, but you don't carry the weight.

That's why cultural cues are critical in Black American genealogy. Our families left signals in the **rhythms of their lives** — the holidays they celebrated (or didn't), the way they folded grief into food and praise, the silence they kept around what hurt too deeply to speak.

You'll see it in the records —

- A grandmother who only ever marked her birthday as *"around Easter"*
- A family who moved their land deed into the church's name to protect it

- The phrase *"laid to rest on home soil"* used across multiple obituaries

AI can't feel these things, but it can help you spot the pattern

PROMPT IDEAS FOR ARTIFICIAL INTELLIGENCE (AI):

When you start tracing cultural patterns across generations, it's not just about tracking facts — it's about listening for echoes. The timing of events, the phrases that repeat, and the ways your family marked sacred time all leave behind a trail. These patterns may not show up in DNA or traditional family trees, but they're just as telling. And with the help of AI, you can begin to detect what was passed down in rhythm, not just in record.

Ask AI to:

> *"List all recorded events (births, deaths, moves) that occur near the spring equinox across generations."*

> *"Identify references to non-federal holidays or religious observances in these family interviews."*

Or Ask

> *"Which phrases are repeated across obituaries in this family line — and what themes do they suggest?"*

This isn't about proving Blackness — it's about **protecting our fingerprint.**

Because every family has a code — and when it's yours, you don't just recognize it…You *remember* it.

YOU CAN'T FAKE WHAT'S ETCHED IN THE SPIRIT

Culture isn't just something we perform — it's something we inherit.

And while others may try to replicate what they see on the surface, they'll always miss what lives underneath: the weight, the rhythm, the memory.

Indigenous American culture was never just style. It was strategy.

It held us together when laws tried to erase us.

It passed down knowledge when schools refused to teach us.

It left breadcrumbs in our recipes, our rituals, our names, and our silence.

AI can't feel the soul of that — but it can help you protect it.

It can trace the trail your grandmother never wrote down, but lived in every pot of greens.

It can connect the jobs your grandfather held to a land-based economy built on ancestral skill.

It can notice that your family always gathered at the same time of year — even if nobody called it a tradition.

It can spot the names that only appear in your bloodline — not on any mainstream popularity list.

It can help you prove what your bones already knew: that this culture didn't come from a textbook. It came from survival.

And survival... that was the inheritance.

You are the keeper of your family's code.

Not because you're gatekeeping... but because you recognize what's real.

And when you **train AI** to see what you already know in your bones, it stops being just a tool — and becomes a witness.

Now it's your turn. Use **[Figure 29]** to map the cultural markers you've uncovered in your family's history. Track the names, phrases, holiday patterns, rituals, sayings, and occupations that show up again and again — and use AI to help confirm whether they're inherited, or imitated.

Because culture isn't coincidence. It's memory — with a rhythm.

And *you* are the one who hears it clearly.

Use this space to jot down any notes from this chapter:

✳ Figure 29: CULTURAL MARKERS TO TRACK YOUR FAMILY

Family Event:

Date/ Approx. Season:

Observed Pattern (e.g. Spring Equinox, Holiday):

AI Notes/ Verification

Figure 29: Culture Code Tracking Worksheet. Use this chart to track the cultural markers that appear across generations. List family sayings, holiday patterns, naming customs, spiritual practices, and repeated traditions. Let AI help confirm what your spirit already recognizes as yours.

FEATURED AI TIP

If you're unsure about a person's identity, AI can help you verify clues like uncommon occupations, recurring neighbor names, or birthplaces. These extra details often carry more weight than just a name.

AI Prompt: "Compare this 1900 and 1910 census listing for a woman named Louella James in Oktibbeha County, Mississippi. One says she's a daughter, the other a niece. What possible explanations could there be for the shift in relationship?"

Part III

Writing the Legacy

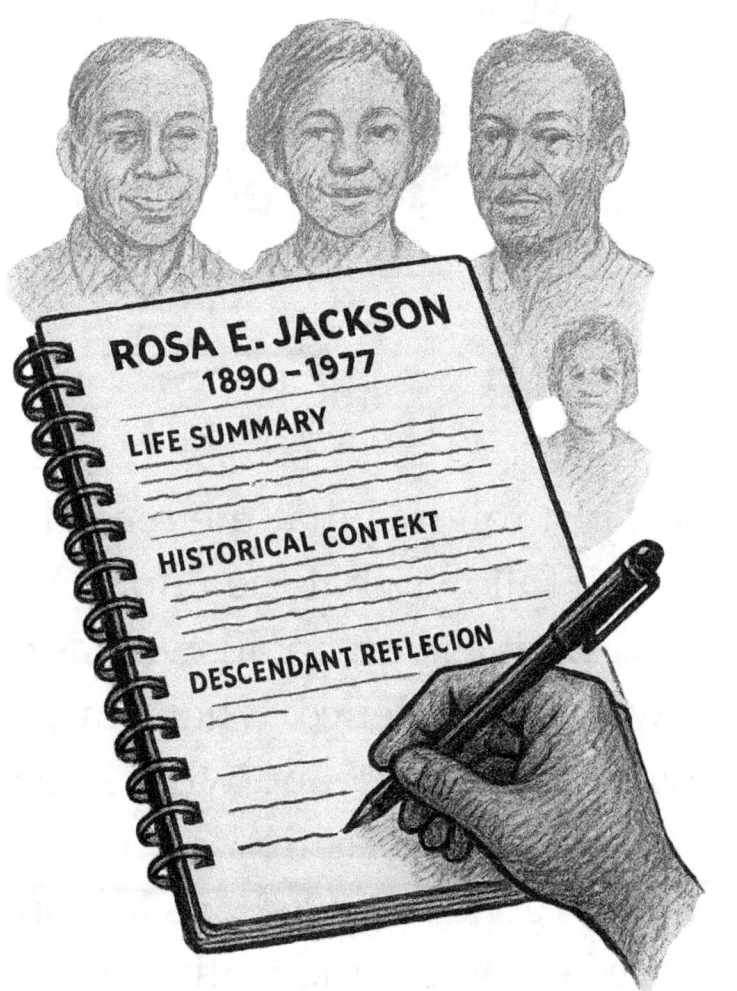

FEATURED AI TIP

Don't just follow what the records say — follow what they don't.

When AI gives you an answer, ask it to show you the silence: what's missing, what's assumed, and what's been reclassified.

In Black genealogy, what's left out is often where the truth lives.

CHAPTER 18

Beyond the Census — Using AI to Explore Land, Wills, and Probate Records

---

Census records are just the doorway. But if you want to understand *how your people lived, what they owned, what they lost, and who they passed it to* — you have to go beyond the headcount.

Land records. Wills. Probate files. Deeds. Tax rolls. These

are the documents that reveal power, legacy, and sometimes... betrayal. They don't just tell you who was in the household.

They tell you **who had a name on the land**, **who left something behind**, and **who got written out of the record** on purpose.

For Black American families, these documents are especially sacred. Because after the slave era, **land was the proof.** It meant self-sufficiency. It meant identity. It meant they could no longer be moved or claimed without paper. Land ownership was more than economic — it was a declaration of presence, of permanence, of being seen by a system that once refused to acknowledge our humanity. These deeds, wills, and probate files tell stories the census never could — about love, loss, trust, betrayal, and who was considered worthy of inheritance.

But here's the catch — these records are often harder to find, harder to read, and buried in county courthouses or scattered archives. That's where AI becomes more than just a helper. It becomes a translator, a scanner, a pattern-finder. It can take the handwriting that used to intimidate you, the legal language that confused you, and help you extract what matters: the story inside the document.

In this chapter, you'll learn how to use AI to:

- Extract names, dates, and property info from land deeds and probate files
- Detect which ancestors owned land and how it was passed down
- Analyze who got left out of a will — and what that

might really mean

- Rebuild forgotten family structures through tax, court, or homestead records

Because beyond the census… is where the inheritance trail begins.

WHAT LAND AND PROBATE RECORDS REVEAL THAT CENSUS NEVER COULD

Census records will tell you who was in the house.

Land and probate records tell you **who built it**, **who bought it**, **who fought for it**, and **who got left out**.

These documents hold the truth that the census often glosses over — not just names and ages, but power, ownership, struggle, and legacy. They show us:

- Who had land in their name when it wasn't easy to do so, and who made wills to protect their lineage
- Who filed claims after losing everything in a fire, a flood, or a system stacked against them
- And sometimes, who had to *fight their own kin* in court just to hold on to what was earned
- Who signed with an "X" but still secured land despite literacy laws
- Who bought land in a woman's name to avoid forfeiture under racial zoning
- Who was listed in estate documents but left off every census
- And who had to reclaim stolen acres through decades of petitioning and proof

For Black American families, these records don't just confirm what we own — they expose what was **taken**, what was **transferred**, and what was **hidden** behind legal language that wasn't made for us to understand.

That's why going beyond the census is more than just advanced research — it's ancestral recovery. But here's the challenge: these records are usually handwritten, old, and written in legalese. And that's where AI comes in — to help you read the parts that were *never meant for you to read clearly in the first place.*

HOW AI CAN HELP YOU READ, EXTRACT, AND INTERPRET LEGAL RECORDS

Let's be real — reading old deeds and probate files can feel like trying to decode another language. And in many ways, it is. The handwriting is faded. The language is stiff. The names are buried between "hereunto" and "aforementioned."

But in that pile of legal phrases is your family's truth — and with AI, you can finally pull it to the surface.

Here's what AI can help you do:

- **Transcribe handwritten legal documents** that are hard to read
- **Identify names of heirs, landowners, and witnesses** in wills and court records
- **Extract locations, plot numbers, and acreage** from deeds and homestead claims
- **Summarize multi-page documents** into who gave what, to whom, and why

🔖 **Try prompting:**

"Transcribe and summarize this 1904 land deed. Who is granting the land, who is receiving it, and where is it located?"

"Extract all names from this probate file and identify their relationship to the deceased."

"List all parcels of land transferred in this document and the counties they're located in."

"Summarize this document in plain language — who inherited what?"

AI won't always get every legal phrase right, but it will give you a strong head start — and allow you to read through the fog to find the facts that matter.

Because every signature on those old documents carried a legacy. And now, you can trace it with clarity.

USING AI TO SEARCH AND DECODE OLD NEWSPAPER CLIPPINGS

Newspapers hold the details that census records leave out. They captured births, weddings, deaths, church meetings, court cases, land auctions, school awards — and sometimes, the truth no official document would say outright. But combing through old clippings by hand can be overwhelming. That's where AI steps in.

You can upload or paste text from digitized clippings — even partial or blurry ones — and ask AI to transcribe, analyze, or summarize what's going on. You can even train it to detect patterns in language, racial coding ("colored," "mulatto," "boy"), and community movements.

Try asking AI:

> "Summarize the key events in this 1912 newspaper article mentioning the Reed family in Randolph County."

> "What does the phrase 'taken up as a vagrant' likely mean in this 1890 clipping, and who might it have applied to?"

> "Search this document for surnames that match my family tree and flag any possible connections."

> "Turn this obituary into a one-paragraph ancestor profile with historical context."

> "Highlight any mentions of land sales or foreclosures connected to Black residents in this article."

> "Are there patterns in how this paper reported on crimes involving Black individuals versus white individuals?"

> "Pull all place names, streets, and counties from this article and map them against my known family migration."

> "Is there evidence in this clipping of someone being reclassified or misnamed across time?"

AI can help you decode tone, identify potential ancestors even when the names are vague, and flag recurring themes — like land dispossession, migration, or social status.

Newspaper archives weren't always meant to preserve *our* stories. But when you pair them with the right prompts, you start to uncover what was hidden between the lines. And sometimes? Those are the richest details of all.

📰 Historical Clipping Example

> Charleston Enterprise: Two or three half-bred negro Indians, who are traveling through the country, struck Thompson's landing this county, about a week ago and pretended to cure any case of disease, and by their talk got horses, buggies, money, silverware, clothing, etc., and then pulled out for other fields. The negroes who got buncoed came to town day before yesterday and swore out warrants for their arrest. The negro Indian doctors have been located at Dexter.

1896

Headline: *Traveling Negro Indians*

Charleston Enterprise:

"Two or three half-bred negro Indians, who are travelling through the country, struck Thompson's Landing, this county, about a week ago and pretended to cure any case of disease, and by their talk got horses, buggies, money, silverware, clothing, etc., and then pulled out for other fields. The negroes who got buncoed came to town day before yesterday and swore out warrants for their arrest. The negro

Indian doctors have been located at Dexter."

AI Prompt to Try:

> "Analyze this 1896 newspaper clipping from The Kansas City Star. What does the language used (e.g., 'half-bred negro Indians,' 'buncoed') suggest

about racial perceptions at the time? What historical or cultural insights can we draw from this article about how Black and Indigenous identity was viewed in Missouri in the 1890s?"

This article may have been written with mockery, but it unintentionally reveals deeper truths. The mention of "Negro Indians" confirms an identity our people have long claimed, while the use of terms like "buncoed" and "pretended" shows how media worked to discredit not just individuals — but entire lineages. With AI, we can now analyze these types of articles for tone, bias, and hidden connections — seeing what was written between the lines.

The paper's tone reflects a wider discomfort with the idea of mobile, self-empowered Negro Indians who operated outside white control. Even in their attempt to mock, the article preserves something valuable — documentation that Black and Indigenous people were known, present, and active in Missouri in the 1890s. It's a reminder that even hostile records can still hold ancestral proof.

THE STORIES INSIDE THE WILLS — WHAT OUR ANCESTORS TRIED TO LEAVE BEHIND

Wills aren't just about property — they're about intention.

They show us who was honored, who was forgotten, and sometimes… who was forgiven.

When you read a will left by a Black ancestor in the 1800s or early 1900s, you're not just reading a legal document — you're witnessing a decision. A choice to pass something down despite the odds. A final effort to make sure that land, livestock, or legacy didn't get swallowed by the system.

Sometimes what's *not* in the will speaks just as loudly:

- A missing name that used to appear in earlier records
- A daughter left out, but her child included
- Land divided evenly, except for the one son who "moved away" under mysterious circumstances

With AI, you can scan these documents for names, possessions, locations, and gaps — then begin to ask deeper questions. Not just what was passed down... but *why*.

Prompt example:

"Compare this will with the 1910 and 1920 census records. Which family members were included in the will, and who was left out?"

"List all items passed down in this will and organize by recipient and relationship."

"Analyze this probate dispute and identify which parties challenged the inheritance. Summarize the case outcome."

AI turns a multi-page document into something you can interpret — and then you step in to read between the lines.

Because this is how we reclaim what they tried to preserve.

Not just the land — but the love, the lessons, and the line.

THE INHERITANCE WAS NEVER JUST THE LAND

When we look at a land deed or a probate record, we're not just looking for proof of ownership — we're listening for the whisper: *"I tried to leave you something."*

Our ancestors didn't always have bank accounts. Some didn't read or write. But they understood value — and they passed it down however they could. Through land. Through livestock.

Through handwritten wills tucked into the pages of a Bible.

Through oral promises that the family tried to honor long after the paper faded.

Some of what they left us was tangible.

Some was stolen.

But some of it... survived in the telling.

Now, with AI, we have tools to honor that intention.

We can read what was once unreadable. Track what was once buried. And give voice to the parts of our legacy that were left out of the census entirely.

Because our story didn't start in 1870 — and it sure didn't end with a headcount.

It lives in every record they didn't expect us to find — and every truth they never wanted us to remember.

Now it's your turn. Use **[Figure 30]** worksheet sample to track what you've found — and what you still need — in your family's land, probate, and inheritance trail. This worksheet helps you document key details from wills, land deeds, and tax records. Use AI to assist with transcriptions, summaries, and name extractions. Let it help you see what your ancestors tried to leave behind — and what it's time to reclaim.

Jot down notes from this chapter below.

_____
_____
_____
_____
_____

✳ Figure 30: TRACKING WORKSHEET

Ancestor Name

Document Type (Will, Deed, Probate)
Year / Location
Names Mentioned
Items / Land Passed Down
AI Notes or Discrepancies

Figure 30: Land & Probate Record Tracking Worksheet. Use this chart to record property transfers, inheritance patterns, omitted heirs, and court disputes. Let AI help you summarize, extract, and reveal the story your ancestor left behind.

FEATURED AI TIP

Names don't always travel alone. Sometimes an occupation, location, or unique household detail can help confirm a match. AI can help you cross-reference unusual jobs, neighbor names, or birthplaces to verify identity.

AI Prompt: "Can you search for records with similar occupations, birthplaces, or neighbors to confirm if this is the same person?"

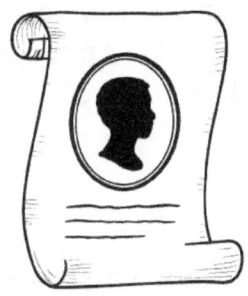

CHAPTER 19

The Ancestor Profile — Using AI to Write Biographies That Honor the Forgotten

---

There's something sacred about taking a census line...

A death record...

A land deed...

And turning it into a voice that speaks across generations.

That's what an **Ancestor Profile** does.

In this chapter, you'll learn how to use AI to turn facts into stories — creating memorials, biographies, and living tributes to the people who made your life possible. For Black Americans, this isn't just about honoring ancestors. It's about **restoring dignity** that was stripped away by systems designed to erase us.

And now?

We're reclaiming that narrative — one profile at a time.

WHAT IS AN ANCESTOR PROFILE?

An ancestor profile is a short written summary — anywhere from one paragraph to a full page — that weaves together:

- **Vital stats** (birth, death, locations)
- **Occupations and family structure**
- **Known struggles or contributions**
- **Cultural or historical context**
- **Your personal voice or reflection**

You don't need a novel's worth of detail. You just need **enough truth to be felt.**

The image in **[Figure 31]** offers a simple guide to help you start shaping an ancestor's story using AI. Think of it like a layering process — each prompt adds another piece of the puzzle until the full picture begins to emerge. You don't need every detail to begin. Just follow the steps, and let the story build prompt by prompt.

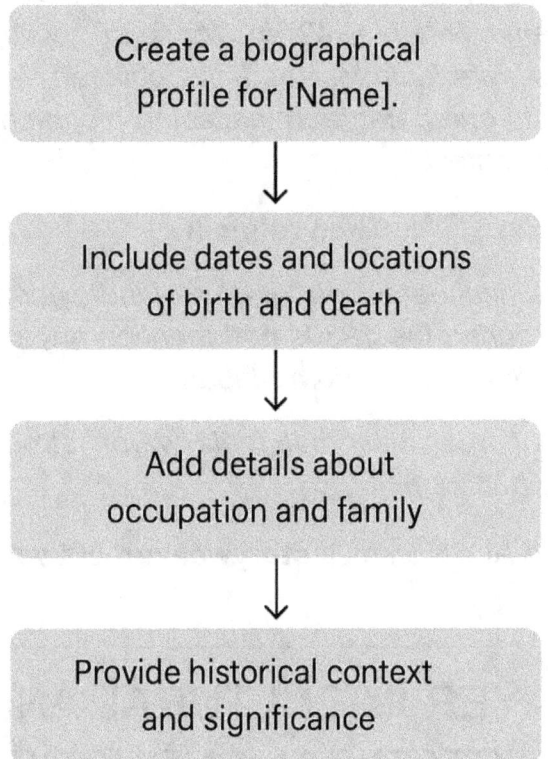

Figure 31: Building an Ancestor Profile Prompt by Prompt. This visual breaks down the process of guiding AI to help you build an ancestor profile. Start with what you know — then use each prompt to add context, emotion, and legacy. It's not about filling in every blank — it's about honoring what can still be remembered.

PROMPTING AI TO WRITE THE PROFILE

Start by giving AI the records or details you have:

"Based on these facts — Robert J. Reed, born 1884 in Alabama, died 1942 in Missouri, occupation: carpenter, wife: Lula M. Reed, five children — write a respectful, one-paragraph ancestor biography with historical context."

Then refine it:

"Add historical details about Black land ownership in Missouri during the 1930s and mention any possible reasons for migration from Alabama."

"Rewrite it in a tone that feels warm, strong, and culturally honoring."

This is where AI becomes a **storyweaver**, but *you* still guide the spirit.

LAYER IN CULTURAL AND HISTORICAL ANCHORS

Dates and names are important — but they don't carry the full weight of a life. To truly honor your ancestors, you need to place them inside the world they lived in. What were the laws around them? The conditions they had to survive? The community that helped them hold on?

That's where cultural and historical anchors come in. When you prompt AI to add context, you start to see your ancestor not just as a record — but as a person shaped by faith, struggle, resistance, and the times they lived through. This is how we bring breath back into the story.

You can also add deeper meaning by prompting:

> "What might life have been like for a Black carpenter in rural Missouri in 1935?"

> "Please Include a sentence about community, faith, or resistance during this period."

> "Were there any laws or events that could have shaped this person's opportunities?"

This allows your ancestor's story to be told **with context**, not just facts.

OPTIONAL PROMPTS FOR PERSONAL VOICE

Add your reflections to make it personal:

> "End the profile with a tribute line from a modern descendant."

> "Include a sentence from the perspective of someone honoring their great-grandfather."

This bridges your voice with theirs — past meeting present. Your reflection doesn't have to be long — just honest. It can be a thank you, a recognition of what they endured, or a promise to carry the story forward. When you speak to them through your writing, something sacred happens: the profile stops being a record and becomes a reunion.

SAMPLE ANCESTOR PROFILE PROMPT

Here's a sample template:

Prompt:

"Using these facts — name, birth/death info, occupation, location, and family — write a 150-word ancestor profile that includes historical context, honors their role in the family, and ends with a reflective sentence from a descendant. Keep the tone proud, respectful, and rooted in Black American experience."

An ancestor profile isn't about embellishing. It's about **restoring.** Restoring the fullness of a life that was only partially recorded. Restoring the richness of a legacy that was reduced to a census code.

This is where the fragments become a fuller picture.

Once you've crafted your ancestor's story using the prompt, you can begin shaping it into a written profile. Use **[Figure 32]** to begin drafting your own — turning names and dates into legacy, and restoring the voice that history tried to reduce.

🌟 Figure 32: BUILD AN ANCESTOR PROFILE — PROMPT BY PROMPT

Use this worksheet to gather details about one ancestor by crafting thoughtful AI prompts. Each section helps you focus your search, identify key records, and build a fuller story — one layer at a time.

1. Start with the basics

📝 *Name, location, estimated birth/death years*

_____

_____

2. What do you want to know?

📝 *State a specific question about their life (occupation, status, family, etc.)*

_____

_____

3. What records might answer that?

📝 *Census, death certificate, land deed, marriage record, etc.*

_____

_____

4. Craft your AI prompt

📝 *Use full context — name, record, place, question*

_____

_____

_____

5. What did AI say?

📝 *Summarize the response or copy important points below*

_____

_____

6. What's still unclear? What's your next step?

📝 *List follow-up questions, documents to locate, or prompts to retry*

_____

_____

Figure 32: Building an Ancestor Profile — Prompt by Prompt: Use this worksheet to build out the story of one ancestor step by step. Each section guides you in crafting thoughtful AI prompts, selecting the right records, and capturing key responses — helping you uncover, connect, and clarify the details that bring their legacy to life.

CHAPTER 20

From Snippet to Story — Using AI to Expand Short Clues into Full Ancestral Narratives

---

Sometimes all we have is **a name.**

Or **a year.**

Or **a place.**

But with the right prompting, that small clue can become a door-way — a portal into an entire chapter of your family's lived experience.

In this chapter, you'll learn how to take the smallest pieces of your genealogy puzzle and, with the help of AI, **breathe life into them**.

You are not just documenting ancestors.

You are recovering **the rhythm of their lives.**

WHAT A "SNIPPET" LOOKS LIKE IN RESEARCH

A snippet might be:

A single census line: *"Sarah Reed, age 32, washerwoman, Mississippi."* A note in a will: *"To my niece Lula, I leave the cedar chest."*

A marriage license with only names and a county

A death certificate with *"Negro"* listed, no parents, and an unfamiliar informant

These fragments may seem small — even forgettable to some — but they hold energy. A name in the corner of a document, a single occupation, a vague location… all of it holds the potential to reopen a forgotten doorway. These are not just leftover lines in the archive — they are surviving threads in your family's tapestry.

And when approached with intention — and the right prompts — AI can help you pull on those threads until the fuller story begins to reveal itself.

What felt like a dead end becomes the beginning of remembrance.

TURNING HISTORICAL CLUES INTO DAILY LIFE

AI can pull from historical archives, local customs, labor trends, and public health records to rebuild her world — not just her role.

This isn't guessing. It's reconstructing the lived truth your ancestors were never allowed to fully document.

Let's take that snippet again:

"Sarah Reed, age 32, washerwoman, Mississippi."

With just that, you can ask AI:

> *"What would daily life be like for a 32-year-old Black washerwoman in Mississippi in the 1880s?"*
>
> *"Would she have owned her own tools or worked for someone else?"*
>
> *"What might her work schedule, community, and risks have looked like during this time?"*

AI can uncover how laundry was done in that region — maybe by riverbanks, in back kitchens, or shared washhouses — and what dangers came with it, like injury, illness, or exposure.

It can surface details like average wages, typical work hours, and even local ordinances that affected domestic laborers.

These insights help you write not just what your ancestor did — but how she moved through the world, how she survived, and what strength that position required.

USING PLACE AS A PORTAL

Even if all you know is a location — say, **Attala County, Mississippi** — you can prompt:

> *"Tell me what was happening in Attala County, Mississippi between 1890 and 1910. Include major industries, Black community dynamics, and any migration patterns."*

Or:

> *"What was the likelihood of land ownership for Black women in that area at the time?"*

Now you're not just listing names — you're creating **anchored narratives**.

Ask AI to compare conditions in two nearby counties and explain why families might've moved.

Search for local newspapers, Black churches, or Freedmen's schools tied to that place.

Find out what crops were grown, what laws were passed, and what resistance took root.

Because sometimes, the place tells the story your ancestors weren't allowed to write.

COMBINING SNIPPETS ACROSS RECORDS

Sometimes one ancestor shows up in four places with only bits of info:

- Census (age and occupation)
- Death record (cause of death, burial location)
- Newspaper mention (brief church event or school honor)
- Marriage index (spouse's last name only)

You can say:

"Combine all the available data about Lula May Reed from these four records and write a short ancestral profile in paragraph form."

AI can weave those clues into a **readable, coherent story** that honors the fullness of her life, even without a long paper trail.

It's not about having one perfect document — it's about making meaning from fragments.

Each piece adds a layer, a clue, a texture to who she was.

And when AI helps you organize the puzzle, you start to see the person behind the paperwork.

This is where research becomes remembrance.

PROMPTS TO PRACTICE WITH SNIPPETS

"Given this person's name, age, occupation, and location, write a first-person reflection based on historical data from that time."

"Build a sample family story for this ancestor using facts from 3–4 documents."

"Expand this one-line record into a full page of cultural and community context."

REAL-LIFE EXAMPLE

Let me show you what this looks like in real time. I started with just one line from a 1910 census:

> ***"John B. Noble, farmer, Choctaw County, age 43."***

That was it. No parents listed. No spouse. No land deed attached.

But I asked AI to look deeper — and that's when the story started unfolding.

It uncovered that Choctaw County had experienced a rise in Black American landownership after the Civil War. It surfaced sharecropping trends, Freedmen's Bureau activity, and even highlighted the economic impact of the railroad. That one census line turned into a four-paragraph family history that I now share in my presentations — not because I added fluff, but because I followed the threads.

And that's the invitation for you, too. Because once you've seen what a single line can reveal, you'll never look at these records the same again.

EXPANDING THE SNIPPET WITH CONTEXT-BASED PROMPTS

Once you've identified your snippet — whether it's a census line, a brief obituary mention, or a marriage index — the next step is asking the right questions to expand it. You're not just trying to make the story longer. You're guiding AI to add meaningful context that honors time, place, and possibility.

The visual in **[Figure 33]** shows how a single line of information can be transformed into a fuller narrative by layering intentional prompts, one step at a time.

Now it's your turn.

Use the worksheet in **[Figure 34]** to practice expanding one snippet of information into something meaningful. Start with a small detail — a name, a date, a burial location, a job title — and let your prompts stretch it into a story. Don't rush it.

Each question you ask is a thread. The more you pull, the more memory unfolds.

Because behind every small detail is a much bigger story waiting to be told. When you slow down and ask the right questions, even the simplest record can open up a world of memory. This is how we begin to restore what was scattered — not all at once, but gently, one line at a time.

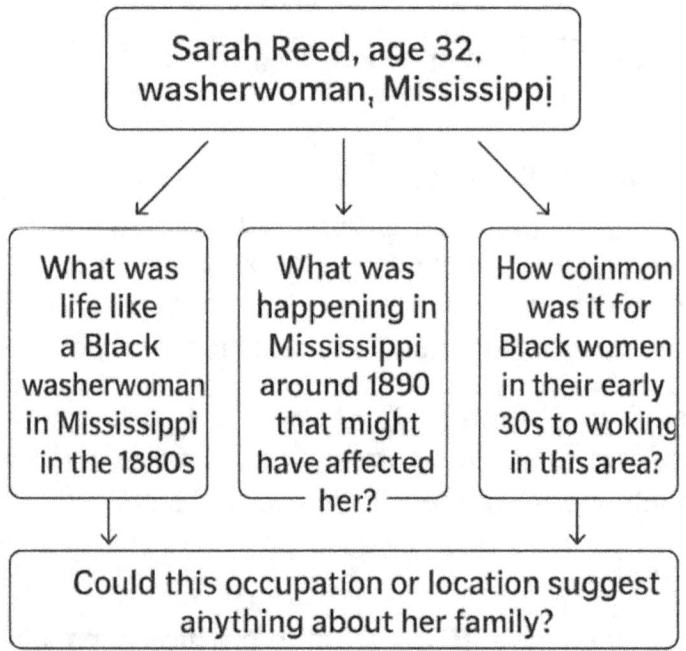

Figure 33: Expanding the Snippet with Context-Based Prompts This visual shows how a simple line from a historical record can unfold into a richer story when paired with layered, intentional prompts. Use it as a guide to turn fragments into fuller narratives rooted in history, culture, and memory.

📝 Figure 34: FROM SNIPPET TO STORY

Use this worksheet to turn scattered clues into a meaningful ancestral narrative.

_____

1. Who is the Ancestor?

Name (full or partial): _____

Known or suspected birth/death years: _____

Race, classification, or misclassification over time: _____

2. Record Snippets You Have So Far

Record Type	What It Says	Notes / Questions
Census	_____	_____
Death Certificate	_____	_____
Newspaper Mention	_____	_____
Marriage Record	_____	_____
Other: _____	_____	_____

3. What Patterns or Themes Stand Out?

Family connections, occupations, locations, repeated names, etc.

_____

_____

_____

_____

_____

_____

4. Draft an AI Prompt

Use what you've gathered to create a research or writing prompt.

Start with:

"Using these facts — name, dates, location, and events — write a 150-word ancestral profile that includes context and ends with a respectful sentence from a descendant's voice."

Or try:

"Based on these scattered records, recreate what a day in this ancestor's life may have looked like — using historical context from that time and place."

"Describe the possible emotions this person experienced based on the events in these records."

"Write a short monologue or reflection from this ancestor's point of view, using facts and cultural cues."

Remember: AI builds the frame — but you give the story its spirit.

Even small details matter. AI can help you connect them — but only you can breathe life into what they left behind.

CHAPTER 21

Twenty-One

Reclaiming Their Voice — Writing Obituaries, Biographies, and Tributes with AI

Some of our ancestors never had a proper goodbye.

No obituary.

No photograph.

No written record of what they meant to the world they walked through.

But we feel them anyway. In our dreams. In our middle names. In the way we pause at certain places in the archives, as if something — or someone — is calling us to look closer.

This chapter is about answering that call.

With the help of AI, you can now write what should've been written all along — stories, tributes, and reflections that bring dignity to the ones who were overlooked, mislabeled, or forgotten by the systems that kept them in silence. You'll learn how to write obituaries for those who were buried without one, to craft full biographies from fragments, and to create heartfelt tributes that reflect the culture, language, and spirit they lived in.

You're not making things up.

You're giving voice to what's already been felt.

And that's the power of this chapter: not to replace the records, but to restore the memory.

WHAT TO INCLUDE IN A TRIBUTE OR OBITUARY

Writing an obituary or tribute doesn't require a full biography — but it does require care. Even with just a few known facts, you can create something that feels whole, respectful, and rooted. The key is honoring both *who they were* and *how they were remembered.*

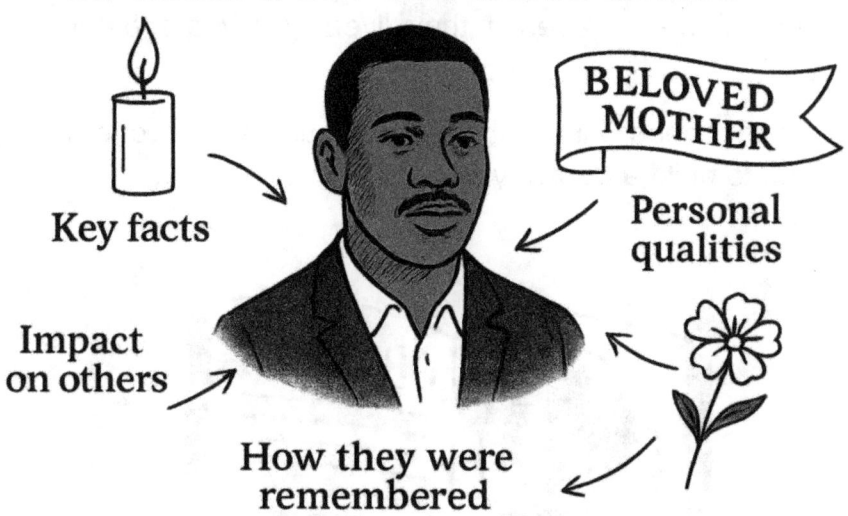

Here are a few key elements to include:

- **Full Name** (include any known nicknames, initials, or tribal names)

- **Birth and Death Details** (approximate dates and places are okay)

- **Occupation or Role in the Family** (homemaker, soldier, midwife, farmer, etc.)

- **Cultural or Community Contributions** (faith, service, music, mentorship, survival)

- **Family Lineage** (parents, siblings, spouse, children — if known)

- **Personal Reflections or Family Lore** (phrases they used, how they moved through life, how they made others feel)

- **Closing Words or Dedication** (honor them from your perspective — even if they lived 100 years before you)

You don't need all of these. Sometimes just one is enough to build a doorway back to memory.

TURNING RECORDS INTO LEGACY — THE STORIES ONLY YOU CAN TELL

There's a difference between knowing your history and telling your story. A family tree filled with names and dates is important — but the legacy comes alive when we start connecting the emotional, cultural, and spiritual threads between the facts.

This section is about using AI to elevate the facts into narrative — not just one ancestor at a time, but across generations. You'll learn how to take census records, land deeds, death certificates, oral history quotes, and migration patterns... and weave them into a story that your family will want to hold on to forever.

Artificial Intelligence can help you write:

- ✓ Multi-generational stories around migration, resilience, and land
- ✓ Personal legacies focused on faith, music, resistance, or healing
- ✓ Narratives with closing reflections from a modern descendant's voice

The difference between a profile and a legacy? A profile says: Here's who she was. A legacy story says: Here's what we endured. Here's what we overcame. And here's what we're passing on.

You're not just writing to preserve. You're writing to transform.

And when you do it with heart and intention — you're not just documenting what was. You're declaring what will be.

PROMPTING AI TO HELP WRITE THE TRIBUTE

Once you've gathered what you know, you can guide AI to help you shape it into something soulful — not just a summary, but a remembrance. The tone you choose matters, so be sure to tell AI how you want it to feel: *reverent, warm, ancestral, spiritual, community-centered,* or *culturally grounded* in Black American traditions.

Try AI prompts like:

> "Write a 150-word obituary for a Black midwife named Lula May Reed who lived in Mississippi between 1870 and 1935. Include her role in the community, her family, and a final tribute line."

> "Based on this census data and family story, create a short memorial biography that honors Robert J. Reed as a respected carpenter and father in rural Missouri."

> "Generate a eulogy-style paragraph for my great-grandfather, using the tone of a Black church elder remembering one of his own."

> *"Write a tribute in the voice of a modern descendant honoring an ancestor who never had an obituary."*

These prompts are not about fiction — they're about restoration.

You're not creating characters; you're reclaiming legacy. You're giving breath to someone who may have worked, raised children, built homes, survived trauma, and passed on wisdom without ever being properly remembered in writing. Let the prompt be a doorway, not a script.

You might be surprised what rises to the surface once you begin. Names you forgot. Feelings that rush in. Visions of hands working, voices praying, music playing from a front porch that no longer stands. That's the power of this process — not just writing *about* your people, but writing *with* them.

Now that you've used the prompts to generate ideas, it's time to move from input to intention. AI might help you organize, draft, and even write — but it can't feel what you feel. That part is yours. This next step isn't just about getting words on a page. It's about honoring someone who may have lived their entire life without anyone ever recording their name with care.

Before you begin writing, take a moment to gather the pieces. The worksheet sample in **[Figure 35]** will help you organize what you know — and what you feel — so you can guide AI with clarity and intention. You don't need every blank filled in. Just start with what's true, and let the story unfold from there.

✳ Figure 35: ANCESTOR TRIBUTE WORKSHEET

Ancestor's Full Name (Include nicknames if known):

Estimated Birth and Death Years:

Place of Birth / Residence:

Known Occupation or Role:

Family Connections (spouse, children, etc.):

Community or Cultural Contributions:

Personal Reflections or Family Stories:

Closing Tribute or Final Words:

Figure 35: Ancestor Tribute Worksheet. Use this guided layout to organize names, dates, roles, and reflections before writing your ancestor's tribute. It's not just a form — it's a space to prepare your heart to speak for the ones who were never given the mic.

Every role held, every year survived, every relationship remembered brings you closer to the spirit of the person behind the record.

Let this worksheet be more than paperwork. Let it be a prayer, a promise, and a powerful beginning to the tribute they deserve.

WRITING FROM FRAGMENTS: WHEN THE RECORD IS BARE

Sometimes all you have is a whisper in the archive — a partial name, an unclear date, a record with more blanks than facts. But even in those silences, your ancestor left something behind. The way they were labeled. The places they lived. The jobs they held. These fragments can still form a story — if you ask the right questions and let your intuition guide what the record doesn't say out loud.

This section will show you how to use AI to turn those broken pieces into something whole. Not fictional. Not filled in carelessly. But carefully reconstructed with cultural, historical, and emotional integrity.

Even a single line in a ledger can speak volumes when viewed through the right lens.

And memory, even when faint, is still a valid source.

The archive may be cold, but your spirit is not.

This is where research becomes restoration.

PROMPTING AI WHEN THE RECORD IS BARE

Even when details are missing, the story isn't lost — it's just quiet. These prompts help you draw meaning from the margins and bring shape to what was never written down:

> "Using only this information — 'Unknown Black woman, age 26, domestic worker, listed in the 1920 census in Georgia' — write a short reflective tribute that honors her labor, spirit, and survival."

> "Given a name and death date only, create a brief eulogy-style paragraph rooted in Black Southern funeral traditions."

> "Build a culturally grounded obituary based on these fragments: no parents listed, died young, worked as a farm hand, lived in Mississippi in the 1890s."

> "Write a 100-word memorial for someone whose story is mostly lost — but whose legacy deserves to be remembered with dignity."

The goal isn't to fill in what you don't know — it's to stretch what you do know into a space that feels whole, heartfelt, and respectful. Let AI assist. Let your spirit confirm.

Even when the records are thin, you can still write with purpose. You might only have a birth year, a county, or a whispered nickname — but that's enough. Because behind every detail is a doorway. A name might lead to a migration route. A single land record might hold the story of a family's resistance. And a burial location might tell you who was honored — and who was hidden. Even the absence of a name can speak volumes when you know what to listen for. These fragments are not failures — they are sacred clues.

Use the worksheet sample **[Figure 36]** to gather whatever fragments you have — a name, a place, a role, a feeling — and begin shaping a tribute that restores voice and dignity.

These small details are enough to begin — because sometimes, what feels like a fragment is actually the beginning of a full remembrance.

Figure 36: GATHER YOUR FRAGMENTS WORKSHEET

Known Name or Nickname

[   ]

Record Type (Census, Death Cert., etc.)

[   ]

Year and Location (if known)

[   ]

Occupation / Community Role

[   ]

Mentioned Family or Neighbors

[   ]

Emotional Tone or Known Legacy

[   ]

Prompt to Help Expand Their Story

[   ]

Figure 36: Writing from Fragments Worksheet. This guided template helps you organize partial details into a meaningful tribute. Use it to identify what's known, what's missing, and how to guide AI toward building a story grounded in truth and care.

REFLECTION: WE WRITE BECAUSE THEY COULDN'T

For too long, our people were denied the dignity of documentation. No obituary to mark their passing. No tribute to honor their labor. No biography to carry their name into the future. But just because the system didn't record them doesn't mean we can't remember them.

Every time you write an ancestor's story — even from scraps — you restore something that was taken.

You rewrite the silence.

You reclaim the voice.

Whether you're working from a full record or a single line, the act of honoring them in writing is sacred. It's not about making history up — it's about making space for the truth that still lives in your spirit. AI can help with the structure. But the soul? That comes from you.

They couldn't write their legacy.

But you can.

And that changes everything.

A middle initial might be your only clue — don't overlook it. AI can help cross-reference initials with full names, siblings, and neighbors to confirm identity.

AI Prompt: "Can you analyze possible full names connected to this middle initial based on time, region, and known family members?"

CHAPTER 22
Twenty-Two

The Living Tree — Using AI to Share, Preserve, and Present Your Research

Research is only half the journey.

What good is a legacy if it stays locked inside your laptop or scattered across folders? The real magic happens when you begin to **share what you've uncovered** — with your family, your community, or even with the world.

In this chapter, you'll learn how to use AI to help **present your findings** in meaningful, beautiful, and organized ways. Whether you're preparing for a family reunion, building a printed tree, or creating a digital memorial, AI can help you transform raw data into **something that speaks with clarity and soul.**

Because when you share what you've found, you don't just tell your family where they come from —

You remind them **who they are.**

WAYS TO PRESERVE AND PRESENT WHAT YOU'VE BUILT

There are so many creative — **and sacred** — ways to honor your research.

- Narrative ancestor profiles **turned into booklets**
- Timelines **that show births, migrations, marriages, and major events**
- Illustrated story maps **that trace where your family came from — and where they went**
- Reunion presentations and keepsakes **to share the legacy**

With **just a little** prompting, AI can support every single one of these.

But presentation isn't just about aesthetics — it's about legacy. What you create now may be the very record someone in your bloodline finds 50 years from now. A name you recovered. A place you clarified. A connection only you could've made. That's why preservation matters.

Consider printing profiles for elders who don't use digital tools. Create a family wall of framed ancestral timelines. Record your own reflections aloud using AI-generated notes as your script. Blend technology with tradition in a way that feels true to you and your people.

Once you've gathered your research and shaped it into family profiles, timelines, or summaries, it's time to make it shareable. This next visual walks you through the process of using AI to create a clear, printable summary that your family can see, hold, and reflect on — not just scroll past.

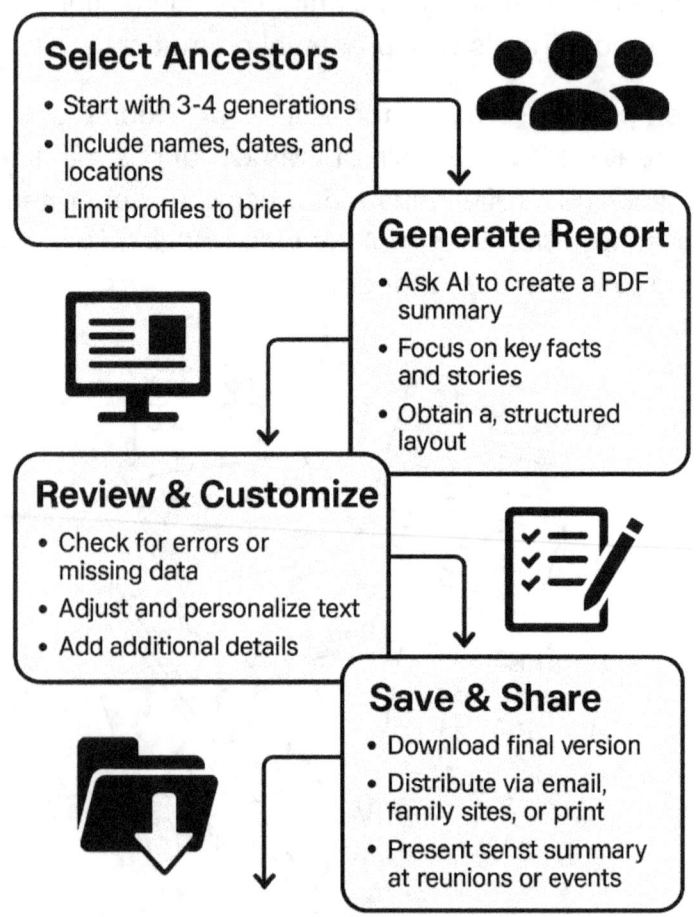

Figure 37: Creating a Shareable Tree Summary with AI — Step-by-Step Process This visual outlines how to prompt AI to help you organize and format your family tree research into a clean, shareable layout. Whether you're printing, presenting, or archiving, this pro**cess helps your findings speak clearly across generations.**

USING AI TO DESIGN FOR PRINT OR PRESENTATION

Once your research starts coming together, the next step is shaping it into something your family can see, hold, and remember. Presentation matters — not for perfection, but for connection. Whether you're designing a keepsake, a display, or a printed legacy, AI can help you turn your hard work into something beautiful, organized, and worthy of the story it tells.

This is where legacy meets layout.

Because it's not just about showing what you found — it's about how you make your family feel when they see it.

And when it's done right, your work becomes more than a report... it becomes a gift.

It becomes something your cousin can hold in her hands and say, *"I never knew that."*

Something your grandchild can flip through and whisper, *"That looks like me."* And something your elders can point to and say, *"That's the story I tried to tell."*

Once you've built your tree summaries, ancestor profiles, and timelines, AI can help you:

- Format your work for print (booklets, posters, PDFs)
- Create slides for presentations or reunions
- Summarize long research into digestible handouts
- Style your visuals with fonts, icons, or color schemes that match your family brand

You can say:

"Create a table layout of my family tree going back four generations, with room for birth/death/marriage details."

"Design a short welcome paragraph for a family reunion program using the ancestor bios I've written."

"Make a printable profile for each of these ten family

members with space for a photo."

AI becomes your layout assistant —while you provide the soul.

SHARING DIGITALLY WITH INTENTION

It's not just about *what* you share — it's about *how* you share it.

The way you present your research digitally can either inspire connection or overwhelm your audience. That's why it helps to be thoughtful in how you deliver your work — making it easy to access, beautiful to view, and inviting to explore.

Once created, you can export your materials as:

• PDF booklets or slides

• Web-ready images

• Blog or newsletter content

• Email attachments or family archive links

And AI can help you prepare all of it.

You can even prompt AI:

"Write an email to send to family members introducing our ancestor profiles and inviting feedback."

Or:

"Please create a Dropbox/Google Drive folder structure to organize profiles, documents, and photos by generation."

That small act of organization might seem technical — but it's actually an act of love. Because how you arrange the story shapes how it's received. It's not just about getting it out there — it's about making sure it lands in the hearts of those you love.

PRESERVATION IS PROTECTION

This isn't just about presentation — it's about **protection**.

Sharing your work builds accountability. It keeps your discoveries from disappearing if your hard drive fails. It lets others add to the legacy, correct misunderstandings, or offer new records you may have missed.

You're no longer doing this in isolation.

You're building something that can live *beyond you.*

A tree that lives only in your mind or your files is fragile.

But a tree that's been **shared, told, printed, passed on** — that tree becomes eternal.

AI isn't just helping you find the roots.

It's helping you grow **branches that reach forward**, into the hands of those who will one day ask the same question you did:

"Where do I come from?"

And because of your work, they'll finally have the answer.

As you prepare to share your work with family or your wider community, this planning sheet **[Figure 38]** can help you stay organized and intentional. Whether it's for a reunion, a memorial, or just preserving the story for future generations, let this be your guide to presenting with care and clarity.

Jot down any notes from this chapter to review later:

_____

_____

✳ Figure 38: FAMILY TREE PRESENTATION PLANNING SHEET

Organize, Prepare, and Share with Purpose

1. What's the purpose of your presentation?

_____

_____

_____

2. Who is your intended audience?

_____

_____

_____

3. What format(s) will you use?

- Printed booklet _____
- Slideshow presentation _____
- Website or digital archive _____
- Social media series _____
- Other: _____

4. Key family members or stories to include:

_____

_____

_____

_____

_____

_____

5. Tools you plan to use:

- Canva _____
- PowerPoint / Google Slides _____
- Word / Google Docs _____
- AI tools (ChatGPT, etc.) _____
- Print service (KDP, Lulu, etc.) _____

6. Preservation plan (how will this be saved and passed on?):

_____

_____

_____

_____

Figure 38: Family Tree Presentation Planning Sheet — Organize, Prepare, and Share with Purpose. Use this worksheet to map out your presentation goals, formats, and tools. Whether you're printing booklets or designing a digital showcase, this helps ensure your legacy is shared with intention and protected for the future.

FEATURED AI TIP

Don't just search for their name — search for what they did. AI can help uncover hidden records through occupations, affiliations, or unique skillsets passed down through generations.

AI Prompt: *"Can you find records for this occupation in this location during this time period — even if the name doesn't appear?"*

CHAPTER 23

Twenty-Three

The Heir's Toolkit — Teaching the Next Generation to Use AI for Black Family Research

What good is all your research if it ends with you?

Legacy is not just about what you uncover — it's about what you **pass on.** And in this era, where tech and tradition can finally meet, you have the power to hand your children, grandchildren, nieces, nephews, or students **a toolkit** they can actually use.

This chapter is about **empowering the next generation** — showing them that research isn't boring, hard, or irrelevant. It's alive. It's powerful. And with AI, it's something they can pick up and carry forward with curiosity and pride.

Because you aren't just building a tree.

You're planting seeds that **can't be uprooted.**

HOW TO MAKE RESEARCH RELATABLE FOR THE NEXT GENERATION

Young minds don't just want facts — they want meaning. So, when you're introducing genealogy and AI tools to them, try to **frame it like this:**

> *"These are your people — not just history."*
>
> *"AI is a tool — you already use it in music, art, and search."*
>
> *"Your family's story matters because you're the next chapter."*

Instead of saying, *"Let me show you old records,"* say:

> *"Let's find out who in our family was a legend — and what they survived."*
>
> *"Research isn't just about the past — it's how you find out what's been waiting for you to remember."*

Whether you're teaching one-on-one or sharing at a family

event, this tool will help the next generation begin their research journey with clarity, confidence, and curiosity.

BUILDING AN AI STARTER KIT FOR YOUNG RESEARCHERS

Every heir needs tools. Not just names on a chart, but the keys to keep the story alive. An AI Starter Kit doesn't have to be fancy — it just needs to be intentional.

Whether you're introducing this to a curious teen or gifting it to a younger child at a family reunion, this kit is about showing them how to begin... with confidence and clarity.

Start with the basics:

- A short family tree — just 3–4 generations they can see
- A printed profile of one ancestor with a photo or story
- A list of beginner-friendly AI prompts they can try
- A notebook (physical or digital) to record what they find
- A safe place to ask questions, make mistakes, and grow

You can even create a simple folder structure for them, labeled by surnames or generations, so they have a place to store records, stories, or notes as they explore.

Give them printed materials they can touch, but also

digital tools they can grow into. Show them how to speak to AI the same way they speak to you: with curiosity, intention, and cultural pride.

You might be surprised how quickly they take to it — asking new questions, noticing family patterns, or even becoming the one who keeps the records at the next reunion. What you're planting isn't just interest… it's inheritance.

Because what you're really giving them isn't just data — it's direction.

And that kind of gift… multiplies across generations

Use samples **[Figure 37]** and **[Figure 38]** on the next few page to build your own AI Starter Kit for a child, teen, or young adult in your family.

✳ Figure 37: CREATING A SIMPLE AI STARTER KIT — A GUIDED INTRODUCTION FOR YOUNG FAMILY RESEARCHERS:

1. Your Ancestor's Name:

_____

Relationship:

_____

Time Period:

_____

2. Start with These Questions:

- Who were their parents, siblings, or children?
- Where did they live at different points in their lives?
- What type of work did they do?
- Is there anything special about their story?

You don't have to answer everything at once — just begin with what you know and build from there.

AI Tools to Try

- Use an AI genealogy platform to search census data
- Ask for the insights based on the location and date
- Generate an ancestor fact sheet or bio
- • Ask AI to compare two records to see if it's the same person

Tips to Remember

- Start with close relatives and work backward in time
- Combining data from multiple records is how you build a story
- It's okay if you hit a dead end — try another ancestor, or ask someone in your family
- Always write down what you find, and share it — even small discoveries matter

BONUS:

If a photo or keepsake exists for this ancestor, print it out and include it in your folder or notebook.

You're not just doing research — you're building a relationship with the ones who came before you.

✳ Figure 38: CREATING A SIMPLE AI STARTER PROMPT

1. What is your name and age?

Name: _____

Age: _____

What makes you curious about your family?

_____

_____

2. What do you already know about your family?

List anything you've heard, seen in photos, or been told:

_____

_____

_____

What's one thing that surprised you or stood out?

_____

3. First AI Prompt to Try:

"Can you help me learn more about someone in my family named _____ who lived in _____?"

Try different versions — change the name, place, or time to see what you can find.

4. Where will you search for records or stories?

- Google _____

- Ancestry or FamilySearch _____
- Newspaper archives _____
- Family Bibles _____
- Other: _____

5. What is one story or name you want to know more about?

_____

_____

_____

6. What will you do with what you find?

- Write about it _____
- Share with family _____
- Add to a family tree _____
- Make a poster or video _____
- Other: _____

7. Who in your family can you ask for help?

_____

_____

Figure 38: Creating a Simple AI Starter Kit — A Guided Introduction for Young Family Researchers. This worksheet helps young researchers get started with AI-powered genealogy. Use it to introduce key tools, spark curiosity, and guide them through their first ancestral discoveries — one prompt at a time.

PROMPTS TO GET YOUTH STARTED

When introducing AI to the next generation, the key is to **spark curiosity** — not overwhelm. You don't need to teach them every

record type or historical nuance on day one. Just give them a doorway, and let their questions do the rest.

Here are a few starter prompts to hand over (or say out loud) to a young researcher:

> *"Who in my family was the first to own land?"*
>
> *"Were any of our ancestors in the military — and where did they serve?"*
>
> *"What was life like for someone named Noble Johnson in Mississippi in 1900?"*
>
> *"Can you build a timeline of our family's movement from the South to the Midwest?"*
>
> *"Can you tell me what might my great-grandmother have experienced growing up in rural Alabama in the 1920s?"*
>
> *"What stories do the women in our line tell — even when the records are quiet?"*

These are the kinds of questions that help young people see the past through their own lens. They turn research into exploration — and AI into a conversation partner.

They might not remember every record or name you found — but they'll remember you showing them how to look. They'll remember that moment you said, "Let's search together." That's how legacy is passed — through presence, not perfection.

And one day, when someone asks them where they come from, they won't hesitate.

Because you didn't just give them answers.

You gave them permission to keep the story going.

And that? That's the kind of inheritance that never fades.

This isn't just about making sure the research continues — it's about *who* carries it forward, and *how* they carry it. Passing the torch isn't dropping a pile of papers on the next generation and hoping they figure it out. It's guiding them, walking with them, and then trusting them to walk further than you did.

Let them hear the stories now.

Let them see your notes, your process, your passion.

Show them that this work is sacred — not because it's perfect, but because it remembers.

Remind them that every name you uncovered was once a heartbeat, a voice, a sacrifice that made their life possible.

This is not just research. It's spiritual recovery.

And when the time comes, hand them the folder, the flash drive, or the printed book.

THE MANTLE ISN'T JUST HEAVY—IT'S HOLY

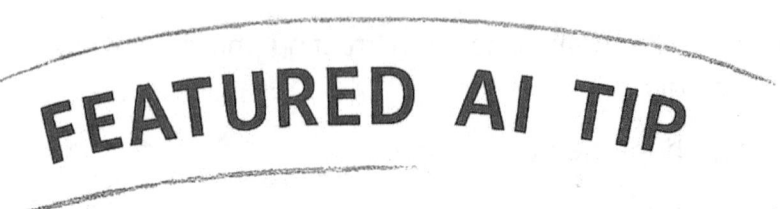

FEATURED AI TIP

"Even when the name is missing, the legacy isn't."

Jobs, places, and patterns can still speak when silence surrounds the name. Don't dismiss the fragments — decode them

AI Prompt: *"Based on this partial record of a midwife in Georgia with an unknown name, what other records or sources might help confirm her identity or community role?"*

CHAPTER 24
Twenty-Four

The Archive We Build Together — Protecting, Sharing, and Teaching What We Found

You weren't meant to carry this alone.

All this research, all this remembering — it was never just for you. It was always about building something our people could return to. A place where the stories are safe. A place where the names don't get lost again.

For me, archiving ancestral records isn't just a strategy — it's part of my Earth's mission. It's also a passion I've carried for years. In 2015, I launched **GriotBooks.com**, a service where I took my clients' records, documents, photos, and oral histories and turned them into keepsake books. I didn't know it back then, but that work was preparing me for what I'm doing now — pouring everything I've learned into these pages to help others do what I didn't have guidance for during my own family search.

This chapter is about the archive — not just a file cabinet or a folder, but a **living vault** of memory, truth, and restoration. It's about protecting what you've uncovered, organizing it in ways others can follow, and making sure that the next generation doesn't have to start from scratch.

Because every census you transcribed, every newspaper you clipped, every obituary you pieced together…

Deserves a home.

Deserves to be passed on.

And with AI, you now have the tools to do just that — not just to research, but to preserve.

Not just to save for yourself, but to **build something we all can inherit**.

You may be the first in your family to build the archive — but you don't have to be the last.

You are creating a bridge across generations.

And when the next one crosses it, they'll know who built it — and why.

BUILDING AN ARCHIVE THAT LIVES BEYOND YOU

An archive isn't just where information goes — it's where legacy rests. If your research is only saved in scattered folders or cloud accounts with no instructions, it risks disappearing the moment you're no longer here to explain it. That's why now is the time to build it with intention. Think of your archive as a map, not a maze. Your descendants should be able to pick up where you left off — not start from zero like many of us had to.

Here's what a strong, living archive might include:

- A digital and/or printed copy of your family tree
- Profiles or biographies for key ancestors
- Labeled folders with records, notes, and transcripts
- A "read me first" file with a simple overview of your system
- Passwords or access instructions if files are cloud-based
- A guide or letter written in your voice to explain why you did this

And if you're feeling overwhelmed, don't worry — AI can help bring order to the legacy you're building. You can use AI to help organize all of this.

Ask AI to:

> *"Sort these folders by surname and create a table of contents."*

> *"Generate a family tree PDF using these 15 ancestor profiles."*

> *"Write a one-page overview that explains how to navigate my genealogy archive."*

The goal isn't perfection. The goal is continuity. You are building something they can step into — and build on.

And remember: it's okay if your system isn't fancy — it just needs to be clear enough for someone else to follow. You're not just saving files; you're passing down a map. And one day, that map may be the very thing that helps a descendant remember who they are.

Even a humble binder or shared folder can become sacred when it's made with care.

Legacy isn't measured by how much you saved — it's measured by how easy you made it for someone else to keep going.

Put your name on the process. Make it personal. Make it yours.

Because when your descendants open that archive, they shouldn't just find information — they should feel your presence.

Let your archive speak like you would if you were still here: with clarity, pride, and love.

TEACHING OTHERS TO NAVIGATE WHAT YOU'VE BUILT

You didn't do all this work just to leave it behind in silence. The archive you've created should be something others can *enter* — not just admire. That means teaching someone else how to move through it, how to update it, and how to protect it.

Choose a trusted family member — a child, niece, nephew, or sibling — and walk them through what you've built. Show them where the records are stored, what the color-coded folders mean, how to use the AI prompts you've written, and where to find your notes. You can even record a short video or write a simple walkthrough to explain your system in your voice.

Here's how AI can help you make the process easier: **Ask AI to:**

> *"Write an onboarding guide for a family member to take over my archive. Include where to find files, how to update them, and what tools to use."*

> *"Create a welcome letter for the next family historian that explains the spirit of this work and how to carry it forward."*

> *"Generate a list of tasks to review and maintain the archive each year."*

You're not just preserving memory — you're passing on a **mantle**.

And the best way to ensure it's received is to hand it over with guidance, clarity, and love.

REFLECTION: THE MANTLE ISN'T JUST HEAVY — IT'S HOLY

This calling we carry as family historians… it's not light work.

We're not just collecting names. We're restoring dignity. We're piecing together what was scattered, erased, or renamed — and doing it with intention.

And now, as you prepare to pass on what you've built, don't underestimate the power of your guidance. Even if you don't feel like an expert, your effort already lit a path. Someone in your line will pick up where you left off — and they'll thank you for not keeping it to yourself.

Because this is more than a hobby. It's a spiritual assignment.

And you carried it with grace.

You did what many couldn't — and what some never dared to try.

You reached back through silence and gave voice to the forgotten.

You restored a legacy that wasn't supposed to survive — and in doing so, you changed the future. This is how the story continues. This is how we remember.

This mantle may be holy, but it was always yours to wear.

WE BUILT THIS TOGETHER

This archive you're creating isn't just yours. It holds the weight of your grandmother's prayers, your uncle's memories, your children's curiosity, and your ancestors' hope that one day, someone would remember. That someone was you. And now, it can be them too.

You've used AI not to replace your voice — but to preserve it.

You've turned scattered facts into stories.

You've turned digital folders into living memorials. And you've built something that will outlive the tools, the trends, and even you.

You honored names that were once whispered and restored dignity where records had been erased.

You broke generational silence with care, transforming research into remembrance — and remembrance into resistance.

What you built is more than a collection of facts; it's a foundation your descendants won't have to start from scratch.

They'll inherit something shaped by truth, steadied by love, and protected with clarity.

This isn't just preservation — it's protection.

So now, make sure they know where to find it. Make sure they understand what it means. And most of all, make sure they know: this archive was built with love — for all of us.

FEATURED AI TIP

Don't Stop at the Census — Go Where the Land and Legacy Live

Before you ask AI to find anything, show it what matters. Your family tree holds the clues — names, patterns, and places. Let that be the map. The search box is just the tool.

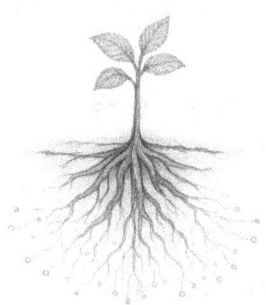

CHAPTER 25

Twenty-Six

The Root Is the Future — Why We Rebuild, Remember, and Rise

You didn't come this far just to trace names. You came to **remember the truth** that was buried.

To reclaim a legacy they tried to erase.

To say to your ancestors, *"I see you."*

This chapter isn't just about wrapping things up. It's about honoring the reason you started this journey — and what happens **now** that the tree is rising again.

WHAT YOU'VE DONE IS SACRED

You took documents that were once used to number, dehumanize, and reduce your people...

And you used them to **resurrect identity**.

You used AI — a tool of the future — to unlock the past.

You didn't let pain or confusion stop you.

You turned:

- Mistranscribed names into known grandmothers
- "Negro male, age 40" into a man with a legacy
- Incomplete stories into whole truths

That is healing work.

THIS WAS NEVER JUST ABOUT THE PAST

Every name you reclaimed was a vote for the future. Every time you said, "My family matters," you planted a seed of healing that moves forward through generations. This wasn't just research — it was repair. It was you saying, "The story will not end with silence."

This work breaks generational curses. It reconnects stolen stories and dismantles labels that were never ours to carry. It brings clarity where there was confusion, and pride where pain used to live.

You didn't just recover history — you rewrote the terms of remembrance.

You made space for voices that were once erased.

You turned a trail of documents into a testimony.

And in the process, it teaches the next generation to walk with their heads higher — not because they've been told who they are, but because they've seen the proof.

Now that you've rebuilt the tree, what you hold is more than a record. It's more than a collection of facts. It's a gift — for your family, yes, but also for your people. You've preserved the legacy… and opened the door for it to keep growing.

FEATURED AI TIP

Don't ignore the neighbors — they often hold the missing piece. AI can help you analyze household proximity, repeated surnames, and shared migration paths to confirm family links.

AI Prompt: *"Can you examine the households living near this person across census records to identify potential relatives or community ties?"*

CHAPTER 26

Twenty-Seven

The Tree Is Rebuilt — Now What?

You did it.

You took fragments and turned them into form.

You also turned whispers into voices, and records into remembrance.

But this isn't the end.

This is the next beginning.

Because when a tree is rebuilt, its roots don't just settle — they stretch. They reach deeper. And the branches begin to grow in ways no one imagined.

WHAT HAPPENS AFTER THE TREE IS BUILT?

Now that your research has taken shape, it's time to ask: *How will this live beyond you?* What you've gathered is powerful — but it's even more powerful when it's protected, shared, and passed on with intention.

Start by preserving what you've created:

1. Back up your files (digital + print)
2. Create a clean copy of your family tree and archive
3. Write down what you wish someone had told *you* at the start
4. Then think about how your research can *serve*:
5. Share profiles at reunions or family dinners
6. Turn key stories into booklets or newsletters
7. Record video reflections for future generations
8. Consider gifting legacy boxes, curated by AI, for birthdays or rites of passage

Make sure your family knows where to find your archive — not just what's in it, but why it matters. Add instructions, context, and even a welcome note for the next family historian.

AI can help you format this into a guide that speaks with your voice, even when you're not in the room. Because research that stays in your laptop is fragile. But research that's planted in your family's rhythm? That becomes ancestral memory in motion.

AI IS STILL YOUR PARTNER

Even after the heavy lifting, AI remains a tool for expansion.

You can continue to prompt it to:

- Track newly digitized records
- Organize your updated folders and documents
- Draft welcome letters for new family historians
- Write ancestor reflections for children to read one day

Let AI keep helping you *tend the soil*, even after the tree is grown.

YOU ARE THE FAMILY HISTORIAN NOW

Whether you feel like an expert or not, you're the one who showed up for the work. And I say that with my whole heart — because I've walked that same path.

This work is deeply personal to me. I didn't start out knowing everything. In fact, I got scammed early on by someone on YouTube claiming to be a genealogist. I learned the hard way that this journey would take more than curiosity — it would take skill, patience, and discernment. So I took courses. I studied. I failed. I got back up. Nearly 15 years ago, I knew —deep in my spirit — I was going to be the record keeper. The Family Historian. The one who would carry the names, the stories, the proof — not just for my family, but for my people.

But it didn't start in a classroom. It started in the house I was raised in — with my grandma, great aunt, and great uncle. They didn't tell me much when I asked questions, but I paid attention. I remembered the little things. And that memory, over time, became my map.

You are the bridge. You are the rememberer. You are the one your ancestors waited for.

And one day, when someone asks your grandchild, *"How do you know who you are?"* — they'll say your name. Because you made sure the story would not be lost.

As a little girl, I used to hang out with an elder who lived next door in a big two-story house. Her husband had passed, and she lived alone. I'd go over after school, and she'd give me ice cream and pound cake while we sat and talked. Years later, through my research, I would discover that she was my grandmother's cousin. That revelation hit different. It wasn't just a coincidence — it confirmed something I had always felt deep down: that I was being prepared for this work long before I knew what it was.

That I had always been surrounded by the very people I'd one day research.

I spent my childhood visiting elders, having sleepovers, going to church with them. I didn't know it then, but I was gathering spiritual breadcrumbs. I was being marked for the mission.

Now, when I sit with old records, I'm not detached — I'm remembering faces, voices, hands that once held mine. I research them with reverence.

So no, you don't need a degree to be the family historian.

You just need commitment. You just need heart.

If you're the one who stayed up late to find one more census record...

if you're the one who asked the same question more than once because something didn't sit right...

if you're the one piecing together what was scattered...

Then yes — you are the family historian now.

THE TREE IS REBUILT — AND STILL GROWING

If you've made it this far, pause and take it in. Not just to be proud — but to be present with what you've done. You didn't just build a family tree — you reconstructed a legacy. You reached back through time, gathered the scattered pieces, and made space for your people to be seen, fully and rightly.

This wasn't just about names and dates. It was about healing what was fractured. About reclaiming what was stolen. About saying, *"We were always here,"* even when the records tried to say otherwise.

Yes, AI helped. It helped you organize, visualize, and fill in some blanks. But it was your spirit that led this journey. Your questions. Your persistence. Your love. That's what brought your ancestors forward and breathed life back into their stories.

Now the tree stands — strong, rooted, and visible.

And just because this book is ending doesn't mean the story stops here. What you've built will continue to grow — in your hands and in the hands of those who come after you.

FINAL CHARGE: LET THE TREE SPEAK

You didn't rebuild this tree for decoration.

You rebuilt it for direction.

For your people. For your children. For your ancestors who kept the story alive long enough for you to catch it.

So, when someone asks you, *"Now what?"*

You can say… *Now, we plant. Now, we share. Now, we rise.*

Because you didn't just rebuild a tree. You rebuilt a future.

So, write the names.

Tell the stories.

Keep the records.

Because one day, someone will say, *"I know who I am, because of them."*

And that "them"?

Will be you.

— *T'Malkia Zuri, The Family Historian*

A family remembering together, with AI as the witness — that's how legacy becomes living.

Rebuilding the Tree
APPENDICES

APPENDIX A
Source Citations

CITING YOUR SOURCES — BECAUSE ACCURACY IS HONOR

You've searched and gathered documents, found ancestors, and reconstructed lineages — now it's time to cite your sources so others (and future you) can follow the trail. Good citations make your work credible, shareable, and easier to build upon.

Below is a quick-reference guide to citing the most common source types, followed by sample AI prompts to help you do it automatically.

SOURCE CITATION TABLE

- **Federal Census Record**

1880 U.S. Census, Randolph County, Missouri, population schedule, Moberly Township, enumeration district 64, page 5, dwelling 47, family 49, John Reed household.

- **Land Deed**

Randolph County, Missouri, Deed Book 32, page 189, John Reed to Robert Jackson, 1905; Recorder of Deeds Office, Huntsville, Missouri.

- **Birth Certificate**

Missouri State Board of Health, Certificate of Birth, No. 4863, Mary Louise Reed, 7 March 1924; filed 12 March 1924.

- **Probate Record**

Estate of Lula May Reed, Case No. 2147, Randolph County Probate Court, 1936.

- **Marriage License**

Marriage License, Robert J. Reed and Lula M. Thomas, 18 June 1910, Randolph County Recorder of Deeds, Book 14, Page 122.

- **Newspaper Clipping**

"Traveling Negro Indians," The Kansas City Star (Kansas City, Missouri), 18 Sept. 1896, p. 3, col. 1.

- **Obituary**

"John B. Noble, 86, Dies After Long Illness," Moberly Monitor-Index, 12 August 1958, p. 6.

👹 AI PROMPT IDEAS FOR CITATION SUPPORT

AI can be a powerful tool when it comes to organizing and formatting your sources — especially when you're dealing with multiple records across different formats. Instead of second-guessing citation styles or searching through formatting guides, let AI assist you in creating clear references.

Use these prompts to get help from AI when formatting or checking citations:

"Create a formal genealogy citation for a land deed filed in Randolph County, Missouri, in 1905 for John Reed."

"Help me cite a 1910 census record for Lula May Reed living in Moberly, Missouri."

"What's the correct way to cite a newspaper clipping from 1896 in Kansas City for a genealogy book?"

"Organize these five record descriptions into full Chicago Manual style citations."

"Generate a source citation for a 1924 Missouri birth certificate for Mary Louise Reed."

"Format this obituary from the Moberly Monitor-Index into a proper citation for my genealogy report."

"Help me cite a Freedmen's Bureau labor contract

from 1867 involving a man named Isaac Thompson in Mississippi."

"I have a copy of a World War I draft card for Robert Lee Noble — can you help me cite it accurately?"

"What's the correct citation format for a marriage license from 1910 filed in Randolph County?"

"Turn these school enrollment records from an HBCU in 1930 into formal genealogy citations."

"Cite a WPA Slave Narrative recorded in Arkansas in 1936 for a genealogy chapter appendix."

APPENDIX B

Glossary Of Terms

This isn't just a list of definitions — it's a language guide for lineage work. Whether you're just starting out or passing the torch to someone younger, these terms will help you move through your research with clarity, confidence, and cultural context.

Term	Definition
Ancestor Profile	A short narrative that honors and contextualizes a relative's life based on documents, memory, and family stories.
Archive	A collection of records (digital or physical) that preserves the legacy of a family or community.

AI Prompt	A written instruction used to guide AI in generating a specific response.
Census Record	A government document that lists information about people in a household during a specific year.
Derivative Source	A document that is copied or summarized from an original (e.g., a typed census extract or FindAGrave summary).
Freedmen's Bureau Records	Documents from a U.S. government agency created after the Civil War to support formerly enslaved people. These include labor contracts, school rosters, and marriage records.
Legacy Narrative	A multi-generational story that goes beyond names and dates to express values, struggles, and lessons passed down.
Primary Source	An original document created at the time of the event (e.g., land deed, birth certificate).
Secondary Source	A document created after the fact that interprets or retells events (e.g., obituary, family

	story).
Snippet	A small clue in research — like a single census line or a name in a marriage index — that can be expanded into a fuller story.
Surname	A family name passed down across generations, often carrying cultural, tribal, or historical significance.
Timeline	A chronological list of events in a person or family's life, often used to spot gaps, patterns, and possibilities.

APPENDIX C
Recommended Reading

Resources to Deepen Your Research and Reclamation Journey

Whether you're just starting your genealogy journey or looking to deepen your understanding of Black American history, these books and resources offer valuable insight, tools, and perspective.

📖 GENEALOGY & RECORD RESEARCH

- *Black Roots: A Beginner's Guide to Tracing the African American Family Tree* by Tony Burroughs

- *Finding a Place Called Home: A Guide to African-American Genealogy and Historical Identity* by Dee Parmer Woodtor

- *The Family Tree Toolkit: A Comprehensive Guide to Uncovering Your Ancestry and Researching Genealogy* by Kenyatta D. Berry

The Source: A Guidebook to American Genealogy edited by Loretto Szucs and Sandra Hargreaves Luebking

📄 BLACK AMERICAN HISTORY & IDENTITY

- *Before the Mayflower: A History of Black America* by Lerone Bennett Jr.
- *They Came Before Columbus* by Ivan Van Sertima
- *Medical Apartheid* by Harriet A. Washington
- *The Half Has Never Been Told: Slavery and the Making of American Capitalism* by Edward E. Baptist

🤖 AI AND RESEARCH METHODS

- *Artificial Intelligence for Dummies* by John Paul Mueller & Luca Massaron
- OpenAI's ChatGPT Prompt Engineering Guide
- FamilySearch AI Labs: https://ai.familysearch.org

🔍 ONLINE RESEARCH TOOLS

- FamilySearch.org
- Ancestry.com   AfriGeneas.com

APPENDIX D

Footnotes

Chapter 1 – Understanding the Landscape

- "Black Genealogy: Basics for Beginners," National Archives and Records Administration.

Chapter 2 – Shift the Mindset

- AI usage and privacy concerns discussed in: Genealogical Computing, March 2023 edition.

Chapter 3 – The Great Reclassification

- Virginia Slave Codes of 1705, Colonial Archives.

- "Free Negroes Reclassified as Mulattoes," The Washington Herald, 1910.

- Gregory, James N. *American Exodus: The Dust Bowl Migration and Okie Culture in California*. Oxford University Press, 1991.

Chapter 5 – Transcribing Truth

- Examples of AI transcription tools retrieved from: transkribus.eu.

- Guide to Understanding Handwritten Records, National Archives.

Chapter 6 – Show Me the Source

- Elizabeth Shown Mills, *Evidence Explained: Citing History Sources from Artifacts to Cyberspace*. Genealogical Publishing Company.

Chapter 7 – Searching Smart

- 1950 Census Enumerator Instructions, U.S. Census Bureau.

- "Genealogical Pitfalls to Avoid," Family Tree Magazine, May 2021.

Chapter 8 – Upload, Analyze, Organize

- "Digital Preservation Best Practices," Library of Congress.

Chapter 14 – Naming Patterns and Generational Codes

- "African-American Naming Traditions," American Ancestors by NEHGS.

Chapter 15 – We Been Had Names

- "Reed Surname in Choctaw and Chickasaw Records," Choctaw Nation Archives.

- Dawes Rolls Database, National Archives.

Chapter 17 – You Can't Fake This

- African American Vernacular English (AAVE) research: Geneva Smitherman, *Talkin and Testifyin: The Language of Black America*.

Chapter 18 – Beyond the Census

- "Black Landownership in the Reconstruction Era,"

Journal of Southern History.

Freedmen's Bureau Records, National Archives.

Chapter 20 – From Snippet to Story

- "Choctaw County, Mississippi: Black Land Ownership Patterns," Mississippi Historical Society.

Chapter 21 – Reclaiming Their Voice

- "Writing Obituaries for African American Ancestors," The Root, July 2020.

Chapter 24 – The Archive We Build Together

- Personal note:

T'Malkia Zuri, founder of GriotBooks.com, began archiving legacy records in 2015.

Expanded List Of Source Types For Genealogy

1. Military Records

- Draft Cards (WWI & WWII)
- Service Records
- Pension Applications
- Freedmen's Bureau Military Records
- U.S. Colored Troops (USCT) Muster Rolls

2. School Records

- Student Rosters
- Historically Black College and University (HBCU) Enrollment Lists
- Report Cards or Yearbooks
- Teacher Registries
- Freedmen's School Reports

3. Church & Religious Records

- Baptism or Christening Records
- Church Membership Rolls
- Funeral Programs
- Tithing or Donation Ledgers
- Missionary or Denominational Reports (AME, CME, etc.)

4. Legal & Court Documents

- Probate Packets
- Land Disputes or Partition Cases
- Lawsuits Involving Freedmen
- Guardianship or Apprenticeship Bonds
- Emancipation Petitions

5. Business & Labor Records

- Sharecropping Contracts
- Employment Ledgers
- Union Membership Rolls
- Freedmen's Bank Applications
- Negro Business League Directories

6. Community & Organization Records

- Masonic Lodge or Eastern Star Rolls
- Benevolent Society Registers
- NAACP Membership Files

- Fraternal Order Records
- Negro Women's Clubs

7. Migration & Transportation

- Passenger Manifests (Exodusters, Liberia Migration, etc.)
- Railroad Employment or Labor Contracts
- Work Permit Transfers Across States

8. Land and Property

- Tax Lists
- Homestead Act Applications
- Sharecropping and Rental Contracts
- Deed Books & Plat Maps

9. Newspapers

- Social Columns
- Obituaries
- Legal Notices
- Articles on Negro Leagues, Pageants, & Local Events
- Black-Owned Press Archives (e.g. *The Chicago Defender, Pittsburgh Courier*)

10. Miscellaneous Historical Collections

- WPA Slave Narratives (with context)
- Indian Rolls and Allotment Records
- School Integration Reports
- Freedmen's Bureau Miscellaneous Files

T'Malkia Zuri

She's not just a trained genealogist — she's a lineage liberator. A modern griot with ancient memory, T'Malkia Zuri digs through dusty records like a spiritual archaeologist, unearthing truths that institutions buried and naming ancestors they tried to erase.

Born in Chicago, raised in Moberly, Missouri — but cosmically connected to a sealed Homeland — T'Malkia is the voice for "Black" Americans waking up not only to their history, but to their divinity. Her research journey began over fifteen years ago, driven by a desire to understand the names and faces buried in her family's past. Along the way, she earned her genealogy certification, built one of the largest archival projects for Black families in Randolph County, Mo., and founded **GriotBooks**, a publishing platform that preserves ancestral legacies in keepsake form.

From radio mics to manuscripts, from the sun's whispers to census rolls, she's been sounding the alarm before the world was ready to hear her. But now? The mic is still in her hand — and the world is finally listening.

She writes with fire, but moves with spirit. Every chapter is a chant. Every document is a drumbeat. For her, genealogy isn't just about records — it's about resurrection. She's the one who remembers — and she's here to make sure you do too.

GRIOTPUBLISHINGHOUSE.COM

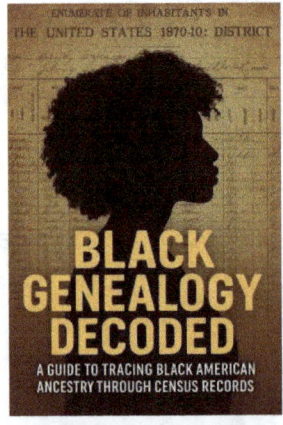
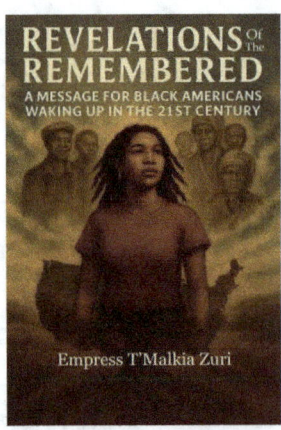
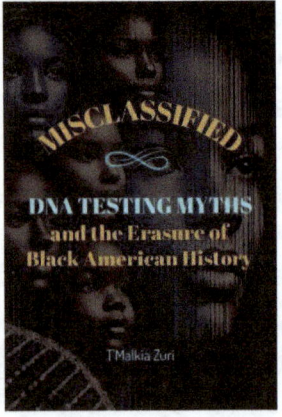
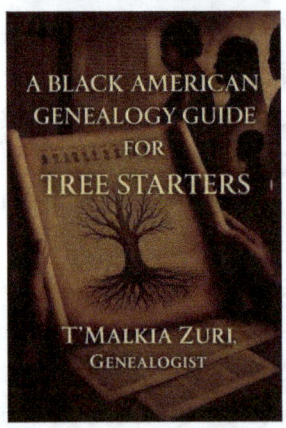